COLOSSIANS

ABINGDON NEW TESTAMENT COMMENTARIES

COLOSSIANS

DAVID M. HAY

Abingdon Press
Nashville

ABINGDON NEW TESTAMENT COMMENTARIES:
COLOSSIANS

Copyright © 2000 by Abingdon Press

This book is printed on recycled, acid-free, elemental-chlorine–free paper.

Library of Congress Cataloging-in-Publication Data

Hay, David M., 1935-
    Colossians / David M. Hay.
        p. cm. — (Abingdon New Testament commentaries)
    Includes bibliographical references and index.
    ISBN 0-687-05802-3 (alk. paper)
    1. Bible. N.T. Colossians—Commentaries. I. Title. II. Series.

    BS2715.3 .H39 2000
    227'.707—dc21

                            99-059736

00 01 02 03 04 05 06 07 08 09—10 9 8 7 6 5 4 3 2 1

MANUFACTURED IN THE UNITED STATES OF AMERICA

To my children,
their spouses,
and their children
for what they have taught me
about love, faith, and hope

CONTENTS

FOREWORD

The *Abingdon New Testament Commentaries* series provides compact, critical commentaries on the writings of the New Testament. These commentaries are written with special attention to the needs and interests of theological students, but they will also be useful for students in upper-level college or university settings, as well as for pastors and other church leaders. In addition to providing basic information about the New Testament texts and insights into their meanings, these commentaries are intended to exemplify the tasks and procedures of careful, critical biblical exegesis.

The authors who have contributed to this series come from a wide range of ecclesiastical affiliations and confessional stances. All are seasoned, respected scholars and experienced classroom teachers. They take full account of the most important current scholarship and secondary literature, but do not attempt to summarize that literature or engage in technical academic debate. Their fundamental concern is to analyze the literary, socio-historical, theological, and ethical dimensions of the biblical texts themselves. Although all of the commentaries in this series have been written on the basis of the Greek texts, the authors do not presuppose any knowledge of the biblical languages on the part of the reader. When some awareness of the grammatical, syntactical, or philological issue is necessary for an adequate understanding of a particular text, they explain the matter clearly and concisely.

The introduction of each volume ordinarily includes subdivisions dealing with the *key issues* addressed and/or raised by the New Testament writing under consideration; its *literary genre*, *structure, and character;* its *occasion and situational context,* including its wider social, historical, and religious contexts; and its *theological and ethical significance* within these several contexts.

In each volume, the *commentary* is organized according to literary units rather than verse by verse. Generally, each of these units is the subject of three types of analysis. First, the *literary analysis* attends to the unit's genre, most important stylistic features, and overall structure. Second, the *exegetical analysis* considers the aim and leading ideas of the unit, deals with any especially important textual variants, and discusses the meanings of important words, phrases, and images. It also takes note of the particular historical and social situations of the writer and original readers, and of the wider cultural and religious contexts of the book as a whole. Finally, the *theological and ethical analysis* discusses the theological and ethical matters with which the unit deals or to which it points, focusing on the theological and ethical significance of the text within its original setting.

Each volume also includes a *select bibliography,* thereby providing guidance to other major commentaries and important scholarly works, and a brief *subject index.* The New Revised Standard Version of the Bible is the principal translation of reference for the series, but the authors draw on all of the major modern English versions, and when necessary provide their own original translations of difficult terms or phrases.

The fundamental aim of this series will have been attained if readers are assisted, not only to understand more about the origins, character, and meaning of the New Testament writings, but also to enter into their own informed and critical engagement with the texts themselves.

Victor Paul Furnish
General Editor

PREFACE

A mong the writings of the New Testament, the Letter to the Colossians has held a special fascination for me for many years, especially since I participated in a graduate seminar on Colossians and Ephesians taught by Professor Nils A. Dahl. The letter's assertions about Christ's positive relation to all creation and its critical openness to both Jewish and pagan ideas and values have struck me as mysterious and stimulating. So I was grateful when Victor Furnish invited me to write this commentary.

My understanding of the complexities of Colossians' connection with other Pauline letters has been immensely aided by the discussions of the Pauline Theology Group and the Disputed Paulines Group of the Society of Biblical Literature. Conversations with members of the Philo of Alexandria Group of the Society of Biblical Literature and the Philo Seminar of the Studiorum Novi Testamenti Societas have enriched my appreciation of the letter's ties with Judaism and Greek philosophy.

I am grateful to several individuals for reading and commenting on sections of the book as they were drafted: David R. Adams (a friend of many years), John Hay (my brother), and Cameron Hay Rollins (my daughter). Jouette Bassler provided essential editorial counsel and encouragement throughout the project. Members of adult classes at Westminster Presbyterian Church and First Presbyterian Church of Cedar Rapids listened to my evolving thoughts about the letter and offered creative responses. James R. Phifer, president of Coe College, and Laura Skandera-Trombley, the College's Vice President for Academic Affairs, were consistently supportive and encouraging.

Linda Bloedel, Betty Rogers, and Harlene Hansen at the Coe library tracked down every book and article I requested.

My wife, Mary Cam, provided inspiration and support throughout the years of reading and writing. Despite my general enthusiasm for Colossians, she convinced me a long time ago not to take too seriously its teaching that wives should be subordinate to their husbands.

David M. Hay

LIST OF ABBREVIATIONS

1 Clem.	*First Clement*
1 Enoch	Ethiopic *Book of Enoch*
2 Apoc. Bar.	Syriac *Apocalypse of Baruch*
2 Clem.	*Second Clement*
2 Enoch	Slavonic *Book of Enoch*
3 Enoch	Hebrew *Book of Enoch*
1QH	*Thanksgiving Hymns* (Qumran Cave 1)
1QM	*War Scroll* (Qumran Cave 1)
1QpHab	*Pesher on Habakkuk* (Qumran Cave 1)
1QS	*Rule of the Community* (Qumran Cave 1)
ABD	D. N. Freedman (ed.), *Anchor Bible Dictionary*
ACNT	Augsburg Commentaries on the New Testament
Adv. Haer.	Irenaeus, *Against Heresies*
Anim.	Philo, *On Husbandry*
ANRW	*Aufstieg und Niedergang der römischen Welt*
Apoc. Zeph.	*Apocalypse of Zephaniah*
AT	Author's translation
b. Meg	Babylonian Talmud, Tractate *Megilla*
b. Sanh.	Babylonian Talmud, Tractate *Sanhedrin*
BA	*Biblical Archaeologist*
Barn.	*Barnabas*
BBB	Bonner biblische Beiträge
Bib	*Biblica*
BZNW	Beihefte zur ZNW
C. Apion	Josephus, *Against Apion*

C. Celsum	Origen, *Against Celsus*
CBQ	*Catholic Biblical Quarterly*
CGTC	Cambridge Greek Testament Commentaries
Cher.	Philo, *On the Cherubim*
Confes.	Augustine, *Confessions*
Conf. Ling.	Philo, *On the Confusion of Tongues*
Decal.	Philo, *On the Decalogue*
Dial. Trypho	Justin Martyr, *Dialogue with Trypho*
Did.	*Didache*
Ebr.	Philo, *On Drunkenness*
Ep. Diog.	*Epistle to Diognetus*
FRLANT	Forschungen zur Religion und Literatur des Alten und Neuen Testaments
Fuga	Philo, *On Flight and Finding*
Gaium	Philo, *The Embassy to Gaius*
Gig.	Philo, *The Giants*
Gos. Eg.	*Gospel of the Egyptians*
Gos. Truth	*Gospel of Truth*
Heres	Philo, *Who Is the Heir of Divine Things?*
Herm. Vis.	*Hermas, Vision(s)*
HNT	Handbuch zum Neuen Testament
HSS	Harvard Semitic Studies
HTKNT	Herders theologischer Kommentar zum Neuen Testament
HTS	Harvard Theological Studies
IB	*Interpreter's Bible*
ICC	International Critical Commentary
Ign. *Eph.*	Ignatius, *Letter to the Ephesians*
Ign. *Mag.*	Ignatius, *Letter to the Magnesians*
Ign. *Rom*	Ignatius, *Letter to the Romans*
Ign. *Smyrn.*	Ignatius, *Letter to the Smyrnaeans*
Ign. *Trall.*	Ignatius, *Letter to the Trallians*
Int	*Interpretation*
JBL	*Journal of Biblical Literature*
JR	*Journal of Religion*
JRS	*Journal of Roman Studies*

JSNT	*Journal for the Study of the New Testament*
JSNTSup	Journal for the Study of the New Testament—Supplement Series
Jub.	*Jubilees*
Leg. All.	Philo, *Allegorical Interpretation of the Laws*
LXX	Septuagint
m. Abot	Mishnah, tractate *Abot*
MeyerK	H. A. W. Meyer, Kritisch-exegetischer Kommentar über das Neue Testament
Midr. Exod	*Midrash on Exodus*
Migr. Abr.	Philo, *On the Migration of Abraham*
Mund.	Pseudo-Aristotle, *On the Origin of the World*
Nat. Deor.	Cicero, *On the Nature of the Gods*
N.E.	Aristotle, *Nicomachean Ethics*
NHC	Nag Hammadi Codex
NICNT	New International Commentary on the New Testament
NIGTC	New International Greek Testament Commentary
NovT	*Novum Testamentum*
NovTSup	Novum Testamentum, Supplements
NRSV	New Revised Standard Version
NTD	Neue Testament Deutsch
NTS	*New Testament Studies*
Odes Sol.	*Odes of Solomon*
Off.	Cicero, *On Duties*
Opif.	Philo, *On the Creation of the World*
OTP	J. H. Charlesworth (ed.), *Old Testament Pseudepigrapha*
Plant.	Philo, *Noah's Work as Planter*
Pol. *Phil.*	Polycarp, *Letter to the Philippians*
Post. Cain	Philo, *On the Posterity and Exile of Cain*
Praec. Conj.	Plutarch, *Advice to the Bride and Groom*
Praem.	Philo, *On Rewards and Punishments*
Pss. Sol.	*Psalms of Solomon*

Quaes. Exod.	Philo, *Questions and Solutions on Exodus*
Quod Deus	Philo, *On the Immutability of God*
REB	Revised English Bible
RSV	Revised Standard Version
Sacr.	Philo, *On the Sacrifices of Abel and Cain*
SBB	Stuttgarter biblische Beiträge
SBLDS	SBL Dissertation Series
SBLMS	SBL Monograph Series
SBLSBS	SBL Sources for Biblical Study
SBT	Studies in Biblical Theology
SNT	Studien zum Neuen Testament
SNTSMS	Society for New Testament Studies Monograph Series
SNT(SU)	Studien zum Neuen Testament (und seiner Umwelt)
Somn.	Philo, *On Dreams*
Spec. Leg.	Philo, *On the Special Laws*
Strom.	Clement of Alexandria, *The Miscellanies*
SUNT	Studien zur Umwelt des Neuen Testaments
T. Job	*Testament of Job*
T. Judah	*Testament of Judah*
T. Levi	*Testament of Levi*
TSAJ	Texte und Studien zum antiken Judentum
TU	Texte und Untersuchungen
Virt.	Philo, *On Virtue*
Vit. Phil.	Diogenes Laërtius, *The Lives of Eminent Philosophers*
Vita Cont.	Philo, *The Contemplative Life*
Vita Mos.	Philo, *On the Life of Moses*
WBC	Word Biblical Commentary
WMANT	Wissenschaftliche Monographien zum Alten und Neuen Testament
WUNT	Wissenschaftliche Untersuchungen zum Neuen Testament
ZNW	*Zeitschrift für die neutestamentliche Wissenschaft*
ZTK	*Zeitschrift für Theologie und Kirche*

INTRODUCTION

THE IMPORTANCE OF THE LETTER

The Letter to the Colossians is one of the shorter writings in the New Testament, but it has played a significant role in the development of Christian thought. Its emphases on salvation as largely realized here and now, on knowledge in relation to faith, on Christ as the head of the church, on the entire cosmos and all humanity as the objects of God's work of redemption through him, and on Paul's authority—all of these pointed in directions in which the church's theology was moving at the end of the apostolic period. Christian notions of ethical responsibility conceived in terms of opposition to asceticism and a kind of adjustment to the outside world, as well as the subordination of wives to husbands and slaves to masters, were influenced by the "household table" in 3:18–4:1. In the fourth century the statements about Christ in Colossians were claimed by advocates on different sides in the Arian controversy, which dealt with the status of the Son of God in relation to God the Father and the created order (see, e.g., Athanasius, *Against the Arians* 2.62-63, citing Col 1:15). In the nineteenth and twentieth centuries Colossians has attracted special attention as theologians and ordinary believers have wrestled with new questions about science and religious pluralism. Because of its assertion of faith's relation to all spheres of life and its rejection of revelation unrelated to Christ, Colossians helped some Christians in Germany in the 1930s formulate their reasons for resisting Nazism (Lindemann 1983, 7, 88-89).

In the first decade of the twentieth century there was a New

England clergyman who once a year preached a sermon on recent discoveries in astronomy. He followed the discoveries himself and the sermon was usually long—forty-five or fifty minutes. When a friend asked him if he thought the congregation got anything from such preaching, the minister replied: "Nothing at all, my dear boy, but it greatly enlarges my idea of God" (Nock 1959, 15). Particularly in its teachings about creation, universal reconciliation, and hidden glory, Colossians has enlarged many readers' ideas about Christ.

The letter was assumed to be by Paul at an early date and included in an early collection of the apostle's letters. Before the middle of the second century, Marcion included it in his Pauline canon, and the Valentinian *Gos. Truth* seems to allude to it more than once (see commentary below on 2:14-15; cf. Irenaeus *Adv. Haer.* 1.4.5). Other Christian Gnostic literature seems to cite it: the *Epistle to Rheginos* 45:25-28 (Col 2:12; 3:1-3; as well as Eph 2:5-6); the Nag Hammadi *Gos. Eg.* 64:4 (Col 2:14). There are possible allusions to Colossians in *1 Clem.* 49:2; Ign. *Trall.* 5:2; *Rom.* 5.3; *Smyrn.* 6:1; *Eph.* 10.2; Pol. *Phil.* 10.1; 12:2; *Barn.* 12:7; *Odes Sol.* 16:18; and Justin Martyr (*Dial. Trypho* 85:2 100:2; 125:3; 128:3; 138:2). Irenaeus is the first church writer to explicitly mention the letter, and he identifies it as Pauline (*Adv. Haer.* 3.14.1), as do Clement of Alexandria (*Strom.* 1.11) and Origen (*C. Celsum* 5.8). Doubts about its authorship were first raised in the early nineteenth century, and in the last two or three decades many scholars in this country and Europe have concluded that it was the work of a disciple of Paul.

It appears that Colossians was somewhat neglected in the early generations of the church, partly because it stood in the shadow of Ephesians. Why, then, was Colossians preserved in the canon alongside Ephesians? One may conjecture it was partly because, while Ephesians refines Colossians in some ways in agreement with early church thinking (emphasis on the Jewish Bible, the church, the Spirit), Colossians contains some ideas not expressed, or not expressed so clearly and fully, in Ephesians: ideas about the relation between Christ and creation, Christ and the supernatural powers, Paul and his suffering, and the hiddenness of Christian existence. Above all, the teaching about a redemption of the entire cosmos already achieved in Christ (1:20) is unique in the New Testament and influenced subsequent theologians (including Gnostics) pondering the relation between the Christian dispensation and the course of the world before and after the birth of Jesus (Schweizer 1982a, 260-77).

Modern scholarly interpretations of Colossians have given particular attention not only to the issue of authorship but also to the "hymn" in 1:15-20, the "false teaching" attacked in chapter 2, and the exhortations related to "household duties" in 3:18–4:1. Sometimes scholars have emphasized not so much what Colossians says as the Jewish or pagan background beliefs and values that may have influenced the letter and, partly because of the letter, the general development of early Christianity. While all such questions are important, this commentary will concentrate on the text of Colossians, how it works as a coherent communication in its present form, and what the historical meaning of the author was as best we can determine from the text.

Who Wrote It?

The issue of the authenticity of Colossians has often been spoken or written about as though it is equivalent to the issue of whether or not the letter was written by Paul. This seems an oversimplification or a misleading use of terms. Whether the letter is authentic in a deep sense is the issue of its truth, the quality or validity of its representation of early Christian faith, and its relation to whatever is real about God, Christ, and the church. The ultimate question is whether it bears authentic witness to the message about Christ, not whose fingers or voice directed the pen. Yet the historical question about authorship is unavoidable and important, both for our overall assessment of the letter and for its impact on how we interpret its contents.

Some scholars continue to defend Pauline authorship of the letter. In the last few decades, however, increasing numbers of others have spoken in favor of its having been written by a disciple of Paul or member of a "Pauline school" sometime after Paul's death. Yet the extensive discussions of authorship, especially in the last quarter century, have not arrived at any decisive criterion on which all or most scholars agree. Statistical analyses of the style of Colossians as compared with that of the undisputed letters have not reached conclusive results (Bujard 1973; Neumann 1990, 217-18). The thought and phrasing of the letter are sufficiently different from what we find in the undisputed letters that it seems unlikely that Paul wrote or dictated Colossians directly. On the other hand, the letter is not so different from the others that Paul's involvement in its composition is impossible.

Many other early Christian writings were, in the judgment of many critical scholars today, pseudepigraphical, including Ephesians, 2 Thessalonians, and the Pastorals (not to mention James, 1–2 Peter, Jude, 1–3 John, and the Epistle of Barnabas). Many writings in the wider Jewish and pagan world were pseudepigraphical. So far as we can tell, the ethos of the environment of early Christianity did not discourage pseudonymous authorship. It is also difficult to tell if moral questions about authorship were raised in the early church. We know that in the later church writings were sometimes denied authority because they were considered to have made false claims to apostolic authorship. But we do not know how serious an issue that was in the first-century churches.

Colossians stands on the boundary between the undisputed letters and the disputed ones. If Pauline, it is probably one of Paul's last letters since it shows considerable development of thought beyond the undisputed letters. If not by Paul, it must have been one of the earliest of the surviving deutero-Paulines. The long list of personal greetings in 4:10-17 can be explained as a device to give verisimilitude to the claim of Pauline authorship. Yet there does not seem to be a similar passage in a forgery from antiquity (Schweizer 1982a, 21).

How is Colossians related to the undisputed Pauline letters? There seems to be a particularly close relationship with Philemon, although there are some problems as well. If Philemon is a resident of Colossae and Paul is unknown personally to the church there, Paul's acquaintance with Philemon must have been established elsewhere. But how can Paul expect that release from prison will lead to his visiting Philemon in Colossae (Phlm 22) if Colossians hints of no such impending visit? The argument in this letter about redemption and release from threatening powers (including "elemental spirits" [2:20]) and obligations recalls Galatians and its arguments against the Jewish law and such spirits. Colossians resembles Romans in some structural features, such as its section of general moral exhortations and its lengthy list of personal greetings at the end. Somewhat similar concerns about wisdom and the Cross, marriage, and the church as Christ's body suggest ties with 1 Corinthians. Ideas about apostolic suffering and God's work of reconciliation in Christ are common to 2 Corinthians and Colossians. To a lesser degree one can find parallels between Colossians on the one hand and 1 Thessalonians and Philippians on the other.

How are we to explain major differences in content between Colossians and the undisputed letters? The idea of "forgiveness of sins (plural)" (1:14) is surely not in fundamental conflict with the undisputed letters, though those letters never use the phrase. Likewise the notion of Christ as head of the church, his body, is not found in those letters, but the *concept* of Jesus' lordship over the church does not represent a gigantic leap beyond the thought of 1 Cor 12 and Rom 12. Some typical Pauline terms like "grace" and "faith" are emphasized in Colossians, but with some distinctive shades of meaning. (The very fact that Jesus Christ is not linked with grace in either the initial salutation or the closing benediction of the letter suggests that Colossians was not written by someone trying hard to imitate Paul's usual letter style.) Overall the letter clearly offers thoughts as well as language about Christ's relation to God and creation and about realized eschatology that go beyond anything in the undisputed letters.

What of the almost total silence about the Spirit and absence of the language of justification and the concern—so pronounced in Galatians and Romans—to define the gospel over against the

Jewish Law? Colossians could be viewed as a striking example of the working principle of 1 Cor 9:19-23, of how Paul communicated with a mainly Gentile audience. Indeed, one could see in Colossians an indication that Paul did not become speechless when he was unable to argue against misunderstandings of the Torah or on the basis of the Jewish Scriptures.

The relation to the disputed letters is even more complex. The Letter to the Ephesians has long been recognized to have an extraordinary closeness to Colossians, and most scholars think Ephesians was written by someone with Colossians on his desk. There are extraordinary parallels of thought as well as language (see Perkins 1997). Parenetic values and the "household table" as well as realized eschatology and emphasis on cosmology link the two letters. At the same time, the ecclesiological focus of Ephesians and its emphasis on Gentile Christians entering on a Jewish religious heritage show that it has different priorities than Colossians. Some general features link Colossians and the Pastoral Letters (concern with Paul's life and authority, use of traditional materials, realized eschatology, opposition to false teachings and asceticism). Yet Colossians betrays none of the concern to define church organizational behavior that we find in the Pastorals, and the concepts of soteriology seem quite distinct although they share an interest in affirming the universal intent of Christ's saving work.

The general prioritizing of realized eschatology and emphasis on affirming ordinary life in the present world, so marked a feature in Ephesians and the Pastoral Letters, is more understandable if the writers of these letters (which also assert Pauline authorship) deliberately depended on Colossians *and assumed that Paul had written it*. Of course those writers could have been mistaken in that assumption, but their use of these motifs—at odds with the undisputed letters—while claiming the apostle's authority is more explicable if Paul was known (or as least widely presumed) to have authored Colossians.

After arguing that the letter is neither Pauline nor post-Pauline, Schweizer proposed that it was written by Timothy in a time in which Paul was unable to write because of imprisonment (an imprisonment more restrictive than that when Philippians was written), Timothy writing "in the same spirit" as the apostle and Paul perhaps adding the closing greeting (Schweizer 1982a, 21-24; Schweizer 1982b, 150-63; cf. Ollrog 1979, 219-33). Other scholars have recently written in favor of this hypothesis (e.g., Dunn 1996, 35-39) and I think it has undeniable merit. We may add to it that Paul, before affixing his signature (4:18), probably had the letter read to him and approved its general content (including the remarkable reference to his suffering in 1:24). This theory affirms a link between Colossians and the historical Paul, though it attenuates the apostle's involvement to an indeterminate degree and assigns the primary configuration of ideas and language to Timothy—about whose thought we know nothing except that we can assume it was influenced by his long association with Paul.

If Paul did write Colossians, he probably wrote it very near the end of his career, probably from a prison in Rome. Despite some similarities with the letter to Philemon, we need not conclude that Colossians was written about the same time. Indeed, the statement in Phlm 22 that Paul expects soon to be able to visit Philemon's household (which must be at least near Colossae) is easiest to understand if Colossians was written at a later point in the apostle's career, and perhaps from a different prison.

On the other hand, it is possible that the historical Paul had nothing to do with the writing of Colossians, that it was written by a Christian leader working in the Pauline tradition, perhaps in an area where a number of Pauline churches were functioning. In recent years a number of scholars have spoken about a "Pauline school" in the sense of a group of church thinkers whose convictions were decisively influenced by contact with Paul himself or his writings (Conzelmann 1979). Or we might think of missionaries who had been coworkers of the apostle. There is no historical reason why Colossians could not have been written by one (or several) members of such a circle of Paulinists. If Paul did not write it even indirectly, the author(s) had a solid grasp and appreciation of many Pauline ideas and turns of phrase and were capable of reshaping the Pauline message to meet a new situation. If Colossians was written after Paul's death, there is no way to decide where it was written or where the intended recipients were located, though one scholar makes an interesting case that the real addressees were Laodiceans (Lindemann 1983, 12-13).

Historical study means balancing probabilities and sometimes living with uncertainty. While almost anything is possible, it docs not seem to me likely that the historical Paul wrote Colossians as directly as he wrote Galatians or Romans. On the other hand, it seems to me about equally probable that (1) someone like Timothy wrote the letter under Paul's supervision and direction, or (2) a Pauline disciple wrote it with no authorization from Paul and probably after Paul's demise. In the commentary that follows, I will usually refer to the author as "Paul," partly since I think Schweizer's hypothesis about Timothy writing under the apostle's authority is plausible, but also simply because the letter presents itself as the work of Paul. But the reader should keep in mind the strong possibility that the letter was actually produced by a Paulinist after Paul's death.

Given this awkward uncertainty about authorship, I will concentrate on trying to explicate the text of Colossians without routinely noting related passages in other Pauline letters. Still, at critical junctures such parallels (including differences as well as similarities) will be pointed out. We cannot ignore the undisputed letters even if we cannot be sure Paul wrote Colossians and must be quite doubtful if the Colossians were expected to have access to any of them. On the other hand, the letter to the Ephesians may be regarded as almost "the first commentary on Colossians" (Lohse 1971, 4; Donelson 1996, 59-60), and it often provides indications of how Colossians was interpreted within a few years of its composition.

THE IMPLIED READERS AND THE "DECEITFUL PHILOSOPHY"

Colossians presents itself as written by Paul and Timothy to a Christian community located at Colossae, a city of Asia Minor.

The letter's closing section (4:7-18) mentions a number of individuals in the Colossian church as well as a number of coworkers of Paul, at least some of whom are known to the letter's recipients. Paul was not the founder of the Colossian church and expresses no expectation of visiting it in the future; his relationship with it is, however, solidly established through Epaphras, one of his fellow workers and a native of Colossae who probably himself established the church there (1:7; 4:12).

Colossae was situated about 120 miles east of Ephesus on the south side of the Lycus River; it was eleven miles east of Laodicea and fifteen miles southeast of Hierapolis, both mentioned in Colossians as having Christian communities (2:1; 4:13-16). The site has never been excavated. Colossae is not mentioned in early Christian writings apart from this letter. Though an important city of Phrygia in previous centuries (see Herodotus *History* 7.30) and a center of the wool and dyeing industries, by the first Christian century Colossae seems to have declined in importance. An earthquake struck the region around 61 CE (Tacitus, *Annals* 14.27) and it may have destroyed the city or at least been a step toward its further decline, but in itself the earthquake does not give a basis for dating the letter. It is not definitely known if there were Jewish residents in Colossae, though we have evidence of sizable Jewish communities in the surrounding region. Coins of the city show that in the Roman period Isis and Sarapis were worshiped there, along with Helios, Demeter, Selene, Artemis the huntress and the Ephesian Artemis, as well as the native Phrygian god Men (Johnson 1950, 6).

What does the letter imply about its intended readers? They are assumed to be an established community, already knowing much about Jesus and the meaning of being Christians. All or most are former pagans (see, e.g., 1:21; 2:13). The names of at least three Christians mentioned in Colossians bear allusions to pagan deities: Tychicus (from Gk. *Tuchē* = Fate), Epaphras (short form of Epaphroditus, related to Aphrodite), and Nympha (probably shortened from Nymphadora, "gift of the nymphs"). Jews and Judaism are somewhat familiar to the readers, yet there is no sign of a struggle between Jews and Christians or between

Paulinists and Judaizers. The implied readers know about Paul and are inclined not to question his authority; Paul explains his authority in 1:24–2:5, but he seems not to have to defend it. In 4:2-6 he assumes that he can count on the Colossians' goodwill. They know many of the persons he names in 4:7-17 and can be expected to respect his instructions and recommendations about them.

On the other hand, the implied readers are attracted to what Paul considers a "deceitful philosophy," against which he strongly warns them. What is the nature of this teaching? An enormous amount of scholarly energy has been devoted to trying to identify the nature and background of this "false teaching." (See, e.g., Dibelius 1975; Francis 1975a; Sappington 1991; DeMaris 1994; Sterling 1999). The wide spectrum of theories reflects both the ingenuity of scholars and the very limited and ambiguous evidence regarding the problematic teaching in Col 2. It may never be possible to gain a scholarly consensus on the identity of the Error (the term we shall use for the teaching attacked in Col 2), and perhaps modern scholars have been more concerned about it than was the author of Colossians (Meeks 1993, 38). Conceivably Paul or the Paulinist who wrote Colossians was not sure of all the details of the false philosophy. For this author, it was enough to stress that Christ was superior since creation to all supernatural powers. Believers who let themselves feel intimidated by such powers to the point of worshiping them or seeking, in relation to them, a better security than Christ afforded, were surrendering their hope of salvation.

What are the essential data that the letter provides about the Error? Its advocates apparently urge that it offers secret knowledge apart from Christ (2:2-3), and they use impressive rhetoric to represent it as a distinctive "philosophy" (2:4, 8). The Error has something to do with "elements (elemental spirits?) of the universe" (2:8) and superhuman beings ("principalities and powers") who somehow disrupt the relationship between humanity and God (2:13-15). These supernatural forces apparently derive part of their power from a "record that stood against us with its legal demands" (2:14)—the terminology is so vague or general that it is hard to think the reference is specifically or only to the Jewish law. Perhaps connected with this "record" is a set of ritual and moral demands maintained by the Errorists: demands concerning food and drink, festivals (new moons, sabbaths), humility and "worship of angels" (a particularly ambiguous phrase), visions, and avoiding handling, tasting, and touching (2:16-23). The fact that Paul does not argue against the Error on the basis of the Old Testament, in sharp contrast to the approach taken in Galatians, is strong evidence that the Error was not primarily a form of Judaism. Probably it was a thoroughly syncretistic movement with both pagan and Jewish components (Furnish 1992, 1092). Paul's urgent warning that this "philosophy" entails abandonment of Christ (2:19) suggests that the Colossians did not see it that way.

What was it about the Error that made it attractive? It must have seemed more sophisticated, offering more knowledge than the gospel communicated by Epaphras. Without openly repudiating God and Christ, the Errorists apparently informed people that there were other spiritual powers that needed to be conciliated or obeyed. They may have stressed spiritual perfection more than forgiveness of sins. The emphasis on "basic" Christian virtues in 3:5-17 suggests that the Error encouraged people to obey ascetic rules that they hoped would lift them above the level of ordinary Christians. On the other hand, the "table of household duties" in 3:18–4:1 might be a response to a claim by the Errorists that they were free from all human authorities.

Paul polemicizes against the Error without implying that the Colossians have actually been seduced by it. He praises their faith strongly and does not accuse any church members of having embraced the false teaching. Yet the vehemence and details of 2:8-23 imply that it is an actual danger, to be warded off as vigorously as possible.

That the Colossians could find such teaching appealing suggests that they felt some dissatisfaction with the gospel of Epaphras. Perhaps they had experiences of moral or spiritual failure that made them think that tightening the screws of self-discipline would remove temptation and guilt. Perhaps they felt that Epaphras should have brought them a higher level of knowledge than they could honestly claim. Perhaps words about supernatural powers apart from Christ made them feel anxious—desiring, like Shakespeare's Macbeth, to "make assurance double sure." The circumstance that many early believers became Christian as members of a household whose head converted (cf. 4:15) must have often meant that "social solidarity might be more important in persuading some members to be baptized than would understanding or convictions about specific beliefs" (Meeks 1983, 77).

At all events the letter implies that the Colossians are earnest Christians, manifesting appropriate tokens of love and hope as well as faith, on good terms with Epaphras, inclined to yield Paul and his message unhesitating respect—and yet that at least some of them are restless, spiritually uncertain, tempted to believe there is a better way.

RHETORICAL AND LITERARY FEATURES

Following an opening greeting and thanksgiving and prior to the final section of personal greetings, the letter offers an exposition divided quite clearly into two main sections, one focused on teaching about salvation (1:9–2:23) and the other on moral exhortation (3:1–4:6). In terms of the main train of thought, one may read 2:6-7 as the pivot of the letter: "As you therefore have received Christ Jesus the Lord, continue to live your lives in him, rooted and built up in him and established in the faith, just as you were taught, abounding in thanksgiving." The entire section 2:8–4:1 may be read as an authoritative interpretation of Jesus' lordship in relation to Christian belief and lifestyle. What comes before in 1:3–2:5 can be seen as setting the stage for accepting that interpretation (identifying the readers and their faith in 1:3-23 and defining Paul's authority in 1:24–2:5). T. H. Olbricht suggests that the best way to describe the rhetorical type or genre of Colossians is to say that it is "continuational" in the sense that the readers are admonished and encouraged to continue in the faith they have already received. Their faith is praised and explained (1:3-20), and then they are warned not to surrender it in favor of the Errorists' teaching (2:8-23). Paul presents himself as prompted by God's commission (1:1, 25) to address them, as well-intentioned toward them (1:9-11), and further commended to them by his greetings and commendations of others (4:7-17) (Olbricht 1996; cf. Collins 1995).

While a unified understanding of the Christian message permeates the letter, there is no sustained argument comparable to that found in Romans, Galatians, or sections of 1 and 2 Corinthians. In particular, there is no argumentation based on the Jewish Scriptures. Sometimes the writer apparently thinks that a short identifying clause suffices to explain or justify his statements (e.g., 1:24: "his [Christ's] body, that is, the church"; cf. 1:27; 2:10, 17, 22, 23; 3:5, 14). The sentences of Colossians tend to flow with a kind of solemn majesty. Often, especially in the first two chapters, they are long, built up with numerous dependent clauses (with heavy use of participles, prepositions, and relative pronouns). Tautologous expressions and synonyms are common, especially in those chapters. This may partly reflect the influence or appropriation of liturgical materials in which convictions are reinforced by repetition.

Sometimes the formulations become murky or awkward, suggesting that they were written under special pressure (this is particularly true in chapter 2, when the writer confronts the Error) and where Paul may deliberately speak allusively because he does not want to advertise the ideas of his opponents (as, e.g., in 2:23). Galatians 2:4-9 offers an interesting example of how Paul's syntax can become tortuous when he writes about memories and issues that are emotionally charged.

The complex shape of its syntax marks Colossians as rather different from the undisputed Pauline letters (Romans, 1–2 Corinthians, Galatians, Philippians, 1 Thessalonians, Philemon). Likewise the letter's vocabulary is distinctive. A total of eighty-seven terms used in Colossians are not found in the undisputed letters (e.g., "fellow-servant," "philosophy," "indulgence," "perfection"), and some terms are given fresh twists of meaning (e.g., "image of God," "fullness," "head"). Colossians contains thirty-seven hapaxlegomena (terms found in no other book in the New Testament); by comparison, Philippians contains forty, Galatians has thirty-one. On the other hand, some terms very frequent in the undisputed letters are used rarely in Colossians. For example *hoti* (meaning "because" or "that") occurs fifty-six times in Romans, twenty-nine times in Galatians, twenty-one times in Philippians, but only six times in Colossians. Another example: *ei* (meaning "if") is used forty-four times in Romans, sixty-four times in 1 Corinthians, twenty-one times in Galatians, thirteen times in Philippians, and four times in Colossians.

It is interesting that of all the letters attributed to Paul, Colossians exhibits proportionately the largest number of textual problems (Metzger 1964, 236). Partly this may be the result of unusual or apparently awkward expressions (e.g., the phrase for "God, the Father" in 1:3 and "the mystery of God, of Christ" [AT] in 2:2), partly the result of the influence of Ephesians on how Christians read Colossians (see, e.g., Col 3:6, where Eph 5:6 has caused "on the sons of disobedience" to be added in some manuscripts).

Many modern scholars have concluded—with good reason—that sections of the letter (especially 1:15-20; 2:14-15; 3:10-11; 3:18–4:1) incorporate traditional materials, probably drawn from early church liturgical and didactic materials. Somewhat like the undisputed letters, which also cite preexisting materials (e.g., Rom 1:3-4; 3:24-26; Phil 2:5-11), the writer of Colossians weaves language and ideas from such traditional materials into the main tapestry of his message. The quotation and influence of such materials might go a considerable way to explaining the linguistic peculiarities of Colossians. In a sense everything looks settled and traditional in the letter, and nothing looks innovative. Nowhere does the author indicate that he is advancing new teaching. In fact, however, a fair amount of the content of Colossians is unparalleled in early Christian literature prior to Colossians (notably some of the assertions about creation and salvation in 1:15-20 and the "household" demands in 3:18–4:1, just to take the most obvious examples). It is part of the style—

or rhetorical strategy—of this writer to present novel extensions of the Pauline message as though they are nothing new.

The last section of the "doctrinal" portion of the letter consists largely of a polemic against a "deceitful philosophy" that would impose new requirements on the Colossians. Even here, however, the author seems more concerned to make positive statements about Christ and soteriology (see especially 2:9-15, 19) than to delineate the false position clearly. It is also striking that no specific opponents are mentioned. (Paul normally avoids naming opponents—e.g., in Gal 3–6, 2 Cor 10–13, and Rom 3:8; 16:17-20—but in such passages he regularly implies that he is urging repudiation of particular persons or false teachers active or known in the community being addressed.)

The parenetic (moral exhortation) section of the letter also for the most part presents positive teaching that is not apparently targeted on any particular church situation (3:1–4:1). This does not mean, however, that moral exhortation is a secondary concern. One recent study argues that the entire letter is best interpreted as an example of ancient parenetic writing, comparable in form to one of Seneca's moral epistles (Wilson 1997, 229-54). This analysis at least demonstrates that there is a practical message connected with virtually every dogmatic or metaphysical assertion in the letter. Colossians does not offer ivory tower speculations about creation, redemption, and the relationship between Christ and God.

In fact the author's primary purpose in writing seems not so much one of countering a false teaching as one of furnishing a compact and quite comprehensive interpretation of the Christian message. A certain "false teaching" was the immediate occasion for the letter's composition, but the letter's content "does not consist primarily of polemic, but speaks to the broader themes of authentic Christian existence" (Wilson 1997, 263). And this presentation is closely tied to one apostle: Colossians deliberately and confidently provides a summary of "the Gospel according to Paul." Although the letter presupposes some previous communications (4:10) and tells the addressees that those who carry the letter can supply information about Paul's situation, the letter seems to presuppose that this will be Paul's only direct communication with the Colossians and the Laodiceans. Paul is the only apostle mentioned, but the letter explicitly affirms the authority of other leaders like Epaphras and Timothy (both may be understood to be Paul's subordinates) and Barnabas (who was once Paul's missionary partner, but surely never a subordinate). Paul asks for the prayers of the Colossians that he may be faithful in his witnessing, but he does not ask for any personal favors or financial support, and there is never a quaver of tone suggesting that he is uncertain or worried about anything—except the well-being of the Colossians.

In keeping with the fact that Paul is personally unknown to the Colossians, the letter stresses his apostolic authority and ministerial relationship with Epaphras and other witnesses, and his sufferings and labors for the Colossians and others who have never seen his face—but not his significance as a possible role model for other believers. Nowhere does the letter call on the Colossians to imitate Paul or follow the rules he has given other churches (in contrast to passages like 1 Cor 4:17; 11:1; Phil 4:9). Paul is represented as a stellar missionary to non-Christians, but for the most part the responsibilities of the Colossian church members are not defined in missionary terms (see 3:1–4:6). Paul in Colossians is above all Paul the theologian, the apostle as reliable interpreter of the gospel and of the situation of the Colossians within God's universal purposes.

The intention of Colossians being thus defined, we may be led to further inferences. Whereas Romans seems largely written as a more or less comprehensive statement of Paul's gospel to prepare the churches of Rome to welcome Paul, Colossians offers no hint that Paul ever expects to visit Colossae. The letter is then no preparation for a face-to-face meeting between apostle and church. Quite the contrary, it is designed to make up for his absence, and assumes that his absence will be permanent. This letter will be in a sense "Paul in the absence of Paul." Why cannot Epaphras supply this deficiency? While Colossians implies that Epaphras's understanding or presentation of the gospel is valid as far as it goes, it may imply that it is inadequate in relation to new questions being raised. Or perhaps the writer thought that the Colossians would like to have a compact summary of Paul's teachings even though they might have contact with other friends of the apostle in the future (such as the coworkers named in 4:7-17).

One notable feature of Colossians is that its author seems to bend over backwards not to expose the degree to which his thought is rooted in the Jewish Scriptures and Judaism generally. Jews and circumcision are explicitly mentioned, and Paul is glad to report that he still has a few Jewish-Christian friends and coworkers. No animus against Jews or Judaism is expressed, and Paul's message is not defined over against Judaism or "works of the law."

In fact Colossians never plainly refers to the Jewish law at all, and no assertion or argument in the letter is based on the authority of the Jewish Bible. This feature of Colossians makes it quite different from letters like Romans, 1–2 Corinthians, Galatians, and Ephesians. There are no explicit quotations from the Jewish Scriptures, and only a few allusions to them. The claims of some scholars to find widespread emphasis on Israel or Israel's Scriptures in the letter (e.g., Barth and Blanke 1994, 64-68, 251; cf. Wilson 1997, 126-27) are not convincing. Nevertheless, Colossians seems to have strong links with strands of apocalyptic and hellenistic Judaism, and its general assumptions about God and human responsibility seem largely rooted in the tradition of the Jewish Scriptures.

Perhaps the author has reason to think his readers will not know or care about the Jewish background of their faith. Or possibly the writer thinks that keeping Jewish connections hidden will help readers better grasp the universal meaning of the gospel (cf. 3:10-11). Modern commentators cannot avoid noting passages in the letter whose meaning is illuminated by ancient Jewish texts. Yet pagan backgrounds must be noted as well. Exegetes should resist the temptation to track down every conceivable biblical allusion or Jewish connection precisely because the letter was evidently designed for readers unaware of, or indifferent to, such associations.

One recent scholar has described the style of the letter as marked by "a delicate touch," with "delicate exhortations that evoke and prod" and "an almost fragile theology" presented with "little sense of hard argument, of proof, or of theological system" (Donelson 1996, 8). There are certainly no long direct arguments, such as we find in Gal 1–4, Rom 1–11, or 1 Cor 8:1–11:1, nor do we find extended defenses of Paul's apostolic authority (such as that in 2 Cor 10–12). Probably the author of Colossians had to tread carefully to claim a right to be heard by a church that had had no direct contact with him. Yet there is considerable indirect argument in the letter, the theological assertions in passages like 1:13-23 and 2:9-15 are more than evocative, the denunciation of the Colossian Error is vehement, and the exhortations and instructions in chapters 3 and 4 are given with no hint of uncertainty. Perhaps partly because some persons in Colossae were raising doubts about Christ, Paul's voice in this letter is confident and direct. Modern readers might wish that his voice was sometimes less assured and definite, notably in the instructions of the household table (3:18–4:1), but it seems part of the writer's rhetorical policy not to appear doubtful on any issue.

Much of the persuasive power of Colossians arises from its presenting a forceful, coherent interpretation of salvation and a straightforward summary of believers' responsibilities in the world, one that points up the folly of the Errorists' position. By alluding to the conversion experiences of the Colossians (especially in 1:21-23 and 3:5-17), the letter seems to seek confirmation in their memories of pre-Christian alienation and post-baptismal empowerment. Even the points at which the author's moral teaching agrees more or less with contemporary Jewish or pagan values probably added to the letter's persuasive power.

Yet, although Colossians offers many apparently clear-cut answers to religious questions, its overall message is marked by considerable openness and an evident intent to stimulate rather than to cut off questioning. It offers bold assertions, for example, about Christ's relation to God the Father and to the cosmos, but it does not go too far in defining those relationships. The instructions about "household duties" (3:18–4:1) seem concrete, but particular questions about application and some household relationships are left unmentioned. Colossians insists that all wisdom is hidden in Christ, but its author does not claim to provide an exhaustive exploration of the mystery.

MAIN THREADS IN THE MESSAGE OF COLOSSIANS

In the first part of the letter, primary emphasis is given to Christ as the mediator of salvation. He is mediator not only of salvation, but also of creation: All things were made through him, and all things hold together in him. His death and resurrection did not first make him superior to all other creatures and powers, but in his death God demonstrated the Son's superiority and the fraudulence of hopes or fears not based on Christ. Through Christ all sins have been forgiven and God's peace extended to the whole world. The Colossians are exhorted to rely on him as the source of their reconciliation with God and the foundation for all their future growth toward perfection. These assertions prepare the way for warnings against a false philosophy that essentially raised doubts about the sufficiency of Christ. Partly in response to that Error, but also on other grounds, the author employs a totalizing rhetoric that repeatedly and emphatically asserts the completeness of the salvation provided in Christ. Colossians affirms both the universality of Christ's lordship and the particularity of the Christian community as that portion of humanity that confesses his secret supremacy (Barclay 1997, 92-95).

The writer makes special efforts to clarify for his readers how their existence and destiny are bound up with that of God in Christ: The gospel mystery is that Christ is among and within them (1:27), they have died and risen and come to fullness of life in Christ (2:9-15; 3:1-4, 10-11), and through Christ's death they have received God's forgiveness (1:14, 20, 22; 2:14-15). The heightened emphasis on Christ in the letter as a whole is balanced by an almost total silence about the Holy Spirit; perhaps the writer of Colossians thought Christology provided a more definite foundation for attacking false ideas than did pneumatology (Schweizer 1973). It is also noteworthy that, whereas the Errorists seemed preoccupied with questions about other supernatural powers, the writer of Colossians mentions them only to denounce that preoccupation (2:8-23) or lay the groundwork for that denunciation (1:15-20). It can hardly be accidental that these supernatural powers disappear in chapters 3 and 4: Now believers need concern themselves with only one transcendent Lord.

The parenetic section of Colossians (3:1–4:6) stresses the hidden life in Christ in the present age. The lives of believers are presently concealed with Christ in God, and they can look forward to a revelation in glory at the end of the world. In the meanwhile they should live by "the New Being" in ordinary daily situations and according to norms that are not always different from those of nonbelievers. It is often in outwardly unspectacular ways that immorality, evil desire, and malice are defeated, just as the old divisions of humanity are peacefully abolished among those for whom Christ is "all and in all." Likewise the peace of Christ is confirmed by the community and extended where believers are guided by forgiveness and love and serve Christ as Lord whatever their social or household positions. Most of the letter's moral directives are oriented toward life within the community of believers. However, the exhortations in 4:2-6 emphasize open-ended relationships with non-Christians, just as Paul personifies the missionary outreach of the early church. The final greetings and instructions in 4:7-18 suggest how the entire message of the letter will be supported and carried further by Paul's fellow workers.

COMMENTARY

SALUTATION (1:1-2)

The opening salutation (1:1-2) follows the normal convention of ancient letter-writing: "A to B, greetings." The formulation of the greetings in terms of "Grace and peace" may reflect Jewish practice. For example, a Jewish revolutionary a couple of generations after Paul began a letter, "From Simon ben Kosheba to Jeshua ben Gilgola and the people of his company: peace!" (Lohse 1971, 5). The formula, "Grace to you and peace," is found, however, at the beginning of all of Paul's other letters ("mercy" is added to grace and peace in 1 Tim 1:2 and 2 Tim 1:2), so there is no need to think that the Colossians would have had specifically Jewish associations with the phrase.

The writer identifies himself as the famous and revered apostle and speaks of being an apostle in relation to Jesus Christ—a leader whose words are to be taken as representing the mind of Christ (cf. Rev 1:1-2) and the will of God. Throughout the letter Paul addresses his readers in an authoritative and official, though always friendly and encouraging, tone. The letter opening apparently assumes that Paul is well-known by reputation to the readers, that they understand the title of "apostle" (used only here in the letter) and that they are not disposed to challenge Paul's right to claim it.

The reference to Timothy both associates him with the writing of the letter and distinguishes his authority from Paul's. Timothy is simply a Christian "brother," just as all the persons addressed in the letter are "brothers and sisters" (v. 2). Though Timothy may in fact have had a major hand in the composing of Colossians (see the introduction), the letter itself makes no such claim for him. The salutations of several other Pauline letters (2 Cor 1:1; Phil 1:1; 1 Thess 1:1; 2 Thess 1:1; Phlm 1) mention Timothy's name immediately after Paul's (exactly the same phrase about Paul and Timothy is found in 1:1 and 2 Cor 1:1). Still, the emphasis of the letter is on the apostle Paul as author, not on Timothy, and the letter-writer will soon shift from "we" (1:3-4, 7-9) to the Pauline "I" (predominant in 1:24–2:5; 4:3-4, 7-18).

Timothy is not mentioned again in Colossians (not even in 4:10-11, where we might expect his name to resurface). Still, the reference in 1:1 would make a particularly strong impression if the Colossians are assumed to know that he is an important coworker and trusted member of Paul's missionary team (see especially 1 Thess 2:7 [where Timothy is even called an "apostle"]; 3:1-6; Rom 16:21; 1 Cor 4:17; 16:10-11; 2 Cor 1:19; later church interpretations of him are offered in Acts 16:1-3; 17:14; 18:5; 19:22; 20:4; Heb 13:23; and 1–2 Timothy).

The persons addressed are described as "the saints and faithful brothers and sisters in Christ in Colossae" (v. 2). This is the only Pauline letter in which the letter opening refers to the addressees as "brothers and sisters" or "brothers" (Gk. *adelphoi*). Perhaps Paul and Timothy want to stress that the Colossian Christians, personally unknown as they were, are nonetheless members of their spiritual family. On the other hand, the word "church" does not appear in the address, just as it is lacking in the salutations in Rom 1:7 and Phil 1:1 (which, like Colossians, characterizes its addressees as "saints").

Holiness, or sanctification, was a primary characteristic of Israel in the Old Testament and the Jewish tradition, and it connotes separation and purity based on divine election (cf. 3:12). A moral dimension cannot be denied, however. Personal and communal purity will be a major theme in 2:16–3:17, and there, too, the writer will emphasize that purity stems from the relationship with God and Christ. This relationship is established in faith;

hence "faithful" in 1:2 probably also implies both the personal efforts of individual Christians as well as solid trust in what God has already bestowed through Christ. The meaning of "faith" will be spelled out at length in 1:5–3:4.

The opening greeting speaks of grace and peace "from God our Father" without adding the phrase "and the Lord Jesus Christ," which concludes every other salutation in the Pauline letters with the exception of 1 Thess 1:1. (Some manuscripts have added the phrase in Col 1:2, obviously because later scribes thought its omission must be a copyist's error.) Given the high prominence ascribed to Christology later in the letter, no diminution of Jesus' importance can be intended. Emphasis on God as "our Father" unites Paul, Timothy, the Colossians, and all who are related to the Father through "his beloved Son" (1:13).

As in many other Pauline letters, "grace" marks the opening greeting and the very end of the letter (4:18). It emphasizes that salvation is a gift God gives through Christ (various aspects of grace will be highlighted when it is mentioned again in 1:6; 3:16; and 4:6; though Colossians never directly speaks of the grace of Christ). "Peace" is commonly used in Jewish as well as Christian letter greetings, and it connotes salvation, not mere absence of outward conflict—a general well-being or condition of harmony between God and human beings as well as within human communities (cf. 1:20; 3:15).

The Christian existence that unites letter writers and addressees is here defined in terms of holiness and peace (terms recalling OT Israel's relation to God) as well as faith and grace (terms especially linked in the Pauline letters with the Christian revelation). Everything depends and grows out of the common grounding of the apostle and those he addresses in the power of God. And just as their identity and origins are briefly mentioned, so, too, is the purpose of their lives: to manifest purity, faithfulness, and peace. These ideas permeate the letter's theological affirmations and moral instructions.

LETTER INTRODUCTION (1:3–2:5)

The first part of the letter presents the foundations on which the direct instructions to the Colossians, beginning with 2:6, are based. This introduction includes a thanksgiving (1:3-8), which is followed by a petition (1:9-11) and a summary interpretation of the gospel message in three sections: a brief statement centered on God the Father (1:12-14), a hymn in honor of Christ (1:15-20), and an application to the Colossians (1:21-23). The entire passage (1:3-23) may also be regarded as an extended thanksgiving. It is followed by a description of Paul and his service of the gospel, which explains his goals and authority as he writes to the Colossians (1:24–2:5). Overall this part of the letter defines the identities of the intended readers and the writer (Paul) in relation to the work and purposes of God. The delay in getting around to the polemic in 2:6-23 suggests that Paul thinks the ground for that attack must be carefully prepared.

Thanksgiving (1:3-8)

Paul's letters often begin with a thanksgiving. In this he follows with distinctive modifications a pattern well attested in ancient hellenistic-pagan and Jewish letters (e.g., 2 Macc 1:10-17). The motif of prayer unites sections 1:3-8 and 9-11, although with this distinction: Verses 3-8 concentrate on Paul and Timothy's thanksgiving for the Colossian church (with particular emphasis on the past founding of the community), whereas verses 9-12 define their petitions for the church's present and future. The prayer is addressed to "God, the Father of our Lord Jesus Christ"—neither Jesus nor the Spirit is directly addressed.

Grammatically the passage is a single long sentence, with a series of subordinate clauses linked by relative pronouns, participles, and the adverb "just as" (Gk. *kathōs* [AT]; used three times). The prayer in verses 3-8 begins and ends with references to the writers—"we" (presumably Paul and Timothy). The main topics mentioned are (a) the faith, love, and hope of the Colossians, (b) the basis for their faith, love, and hope in the true gospel, which is gaining adherents throughout the world, and (c) the ways in which Paul and Timothy, Epaphras, and the Colossians are connected with one another. This Thanksgiving section thus prepares the reader for the letter's statements about the content of the Christian message in 1:12-23 and about Paul's authority in 1:24–2:5. The polemic of 2:6-23 is hinted at: The Colossians need to stick with the true message as previously communicated by Epaphras and now interpreted by Paul. Finally, various facets of Christian love are laid out in the hortatory section, 3:1–4:6. Thus the thanksgiving paragraph signals the major themes of the entire letter.

◊   ◊   ◊   ◊

Paul and Timothy introduce themselves to the congregation by saying that they regularly give thanks to God for the church. Since this letter was meant to be read publicly in the church at Colossae (4:16), the prayers mentioned here are linked to the prayers of that church and Paul's request that the church pray for him and his mission (4:2-4). Later Epaphras is described as praying continually for the Colossians (4:12).

The thanksgiving proceeds to praise the Colossians indirectly because they actually manifest primary Christian virtues and thereby stand on solid ground. The triad of faith, love, and hope dominate verses 4-5 (cf. 1 Thess 1:3; 5:8; 1 Cor 13:13; Gal 5:5-6). These Christian excellences are grounded in the "word of the truth, the gospel," which has come to the Colossians just as it is being fruitfully proclaimed "in the whole world."

Faith, love, and hope are each qualified or defined. First is "your faith," which is "in" Christ Jesus. Then comes love, which is directed "for all the saints" (i.e., toward fellow Christians). Finally there is hope, which is "laid up for you in heaven."

The writer speaks here of faith "in" (Gk. *en*) Christ Jesus, just as in 2:5 he will speak of faith "in" (Gk. *eis*) Christ. Neither formulation is found in the undisputed letters (unless Gal 3:26 means to refer to faith "in" Christ). How faith is oriented to Christ and to God is not specified here—faith's full meaning will become clearer as the letter proceeds.

Is Christian love here assumed to be directed only to other Christians? The concern for missionary witness to outsiders expressed elsewhere in the letter implies a negative answer. Yet the love especially in view in verse 4 is directed toward fellow church members (as in Gal 5:14; 1 Thess 4:9; Phlm 5; cf. 1 Pet 2:17; John 13:34-35; 15:17; 1 John 4:7, 20-21).

The Colossians' faith and love, according to verse 5, are based on "the hope laid up for you in heaven. You have heard of this hope before in the word of the truth, the gospel." This need not be taken crassly to mean that the Colossians display faith and love in order to earn a reward in the future, but rather that faith and love as well as hope are based on a transcendent treasure announced in the gospel. Future eschatology is strongly expressed here and in a few other places in Colossians, but the letter says nothing about how near the end of the world may be. References to the future hope of salvation are found in the opening sections of other Pauline letters, notably 1 Cor 1:7-8; Phil 1:6; 2 Thess 1:6-10; but in all of these reference is made to "the day" of the Lord Jesus, a phrase not found in Colossians (cf. Eph 1:3, 14, 18; 2 Tim 1:12, 18).

A similar formulation concerning the eschatological hope is found in 1 Pet 1:4 ("an inheritance that is imperishable, undefiled, and unfading, kept in heaven for you, who are being protected by the power of God through faith for a salvation ready to be revealed in the last time"). The idea of an already-established heavenly treasure recalls Matt 25:34 ("the kingdom prepared for you from the foundation of the world"). The concept of divine rewards prepared for the righteous is attested in Philo's *Praem.* 104 as well as in apocalyptic texts like *2 Apoc. Bar.* 14:12; 24:1 and 4 Ezra 7:14.

Just as the treasure is "laid up" securely in heaven, so also the hope is based on a true communication, the Christian gospel about salvation through Jesus, which is a statement about what God has accomplished ("the grace of God"—v. 6). Its content (or goal) may even be designated as "the kingdom of God" (4:11). The stress on truth in verses 5, 6 implies that the message the Colossians have accepted is fully reliable and that they should be on their guard against alternative messages (see also 2 Cor 4:2; 6:7; Gal 2:5, 14; 5:7).

There may be some deliberate contrast between the hope that is deferred and the word that is already present (Gk. *parontos eis hymas;* 1:6). Rather than speaking of the church community or the world Christian population growing as people make faith decisions, Colossians speaks of the divine word bearing fruit and growing throughout the world—implying that the initiative or power comes from God. It is conceivable that there is also an allusion here to Jesus' parables of growth (Mark 4 par.), where the kingdom of God, represented by the seed, grows mysteriously and bountifully (cf. the use of the metaphor in Acts 6:7; 12:24; 13:49; 19:20). Colossians 1:6-8 also recalls 1 Cor 3:5-10, where Paul, speaking of the Corinthian church, describes Apollos and himself as equal servants who planted and watered while "God gave the growth" and also hints of an argument later taken up by Augustine: The worldwide diffusion of the Christian message is evidence of its truth (*Confes.* 6.11). The use of the terms "bearing fruit" and "growing" is the first instance of a major stylistic feature of Colossians, the use of repetitious phrasing for emphasis.

Verse 7 indicates that Epaphras first brought the gospel to Colossae and was responsible for founding the church there. More recently (v. 8) he has informed Paul and Timothy about the church's situation and its "love in the Spirit," prompting them to write this letter. Epaphras is mentioned again in 4:12, near the end of the letter; the location of these references to Ephaphras may be intended to imply that Paul writes with Epaphras at his side, probably advising the apostle on what issues to treat, praying for the Colossians that they may "stand mature and fully assured in everything that God wills" (4:12-13)—exactly what Paul will pray for them in 1:9-12 (cf. 1:28-29).

This verse offers something like a self-correction. Epaphras is first described as "our beloved fellow servant" (Gk. *sundoulos*), but then as a faithful minister or servant (Gk. *diakonos*) in the service of Christ "on our behalf" (i.e., on behalf of Paul and Timothy; some manuscripts, preferred by the NRSV, read "on your behalf"). He is a coworker with Paul and Timothy, but his master is Christ. The language of serving Christ for the good of others points toward the teachings about slavery in a Christian household (3:22–4:1) and may allude to the background of Onesimus (4:9). The Colossians have already shown their confidence in the message of Epaphras. Since Paul and Timothy are his colleagues in Christ's service, what they will now proceed to say to the Colossians also merits their attention.

Can anything more be inferred about the relation of Epaphras to the Colossians on the one hand and to Paul on the other? Is he a member of a Pauline missionary "team"? Did he found the Colossian church at Paul's direction and under his supervision? Lohse concludes that Epaphras is the authorized representative of Paul in Colossae, since Paul as apostle to the Gentiles is also responsible for Colossae (Lohse 1971, 23). This is at least a good possibility.

The last word in verse 8 is "Spirit" (Gk. *pneuma*). It occurs only here and in 2:5 ("though I am absent in body, I am with you in spirit"). The adjective "spiritual" occurs in 1:9 and 3:16. Colossians has virtually nothing to say about the Holy Spirit, though the Spirit is mentioned very often in the undisputed letters. For reasons to be discussed later, the opponents attacked in 2:8-23 may have stressed the Spirit and deemphasized Christ; the writer of Colossians does the reverse. The "love in the Spirit" or "spiritual love" reported by Epaphras means probably both Christian love in general and love and respect directed specifically toward Paul and Timothy.

Intercession (1:9-11)

Verses 9-20 form a single sentence, its complex clauses joined largely by means of participles in verses 9-12 and by pronominal constructions in verses 13-20. This passage in turn may be viewed as an extension of the thanksgiving begun in verse 3 (note the "giving thanks" in v. 12). Whereas 1:3-8 concentrate on the present spiritual success of the Colossian church and its basis in the divine Word, verses 9-11 focus on the church's spiritual needs, diplomatically presented as a report of prayers Paul and Timothy regularly offer for the Colossian believers. Thanksgiving and exhortation are closely associated in the Pauline letters (Schubert 1939, 87-89). The principal need of the Colossians is here identified as a need for a fuller understanding of God's will, which will prompt appropriate living. This prepares readers for the next section, which defines the will of God as made known in the message about Christ (vv. 12-23).

The passage is marked by several repetitious expressions: "praying for . . . and asking" (v. 9), "knowledge . . . wisdom and understanding" (v. 9), "made strong with all the strength that comes from his glorious power" (v. 11). Such redundancy may strike a modern reader as tedious, but it could impress ancient readers as offering a kind of rhetorical elegance; repetition or the use of near-synonyms also underlines the importance the writer(s) give to defining the needs of the Colossians. On the other hand, the fivefold use of the Greek word meaning "all" (Gk. *pas*) in verses 9-11 implies that Paul and Timothy are sure that God can and will give the Colossians everything they need (cf. the frequent use of "all" in 1:15-20).

◊ ◊ ◊ ◊

A reference to what the writers have already heard about the Colossians links verse 9 with verses 4 and 8. Verse 9 also repeats the assurance that Paul and Timothy pray regularly for the welfare of the church (cf. v. 3). What the Colossians need above all is "knowledge . . . in all spiritual wisdom and understanding." The knowledge needed by the Colossians (Gk. *epignōsis*—the term is used twice in vv. 9-10) is essentially knowledge about God and God's will for their lives. It is not clear that any precise distinctions are in mind between "knowledge," "wisdom" (Gk. *sophia*), and "spiritual understanding," though the last term suggests knowing with insight—probably hinting at the Colossian Christians' need to identify and reject what 2:8 calls "philosophy and empty deceit." Their attention should be concentrated on "walking" (living) so as to be "worthy" of the Lord. The "Lord" mentioned in verse 10 may be God the Father, but the term is usually applied to Christ in this letter, so that is probably the reference here. The idea of worthiness seems close to "as is fitting in the Lord" in 3:18 or "fearing the Lord" (3:22) or "do[ing] everything in the name of the Lord Jesus" in 3:17. The notion that believers should "lead lives worthy of the Lord" probably reflects a Jewish tradition going back to Enoch (e.g., Gen 5:22, 24; Ps 69:31; Prov 16:7; Isa 56:4; 66:4; Mic 6:7; Mal 1:8; 1 Cor 7:32; 2 Cor 5:9; Phil 4:18; 1 Thess 2:4; Heb 11:5; Wis 4:10, 14; 9:9-10; Sir 2:6; 35:5, 20; 44:16; 50:15; Tob 3:15; 14:8-9; Bar 4:4; Philo *Fuga* 88, *Opif.* 144). The knowledge for which the writers pray is not speculative or the kind of esoteric understanding sometimes extolled by apocalyptic or Gnostic writers; the knowledge sought here is knowledge of God's will that issues in daily obedience.

To do the will of God it is necessary to discern the will of God—and Paul and Timothy imply that this requires divine illumination. The Colossians already know about Christ in faith and demonstrate love, and yet they require further enlightenment. The statement in verse 10 that the Colossians need to bear fruit (through performing every good work) and grow in the knowledge of God recalls the statement in verse 6 that the word of the gospel is bearing fruit and growing in the entire world. This similarity suggests that their good conduct will recommend that gospel to outsiders: The Word of the gospel that is the source of their life and good conduct will bear fruit by converting non-Christians. Yet the fruit-bearing and growth in knowledge in center focus in verse 10 take place within the church. Hellenistic Judaism often spoke of growth in wisdom producing the fruit of virtue (e.g. Philo *Cher.* 84; *Gig.* 4; *Vita Mos.* 2.66).

The emphasis in verse 11 on divine power implies a close linkage between knowledge and power: Through knowledge the Colossians will gain the strength they need, through power they will be able to put their knowledge into effect. Yet this power is to be demonstrated now within the church in the form of endurance and patience. The term referring to "endurance" occurs only here in Colossians. Elsewhere the letter will speak of the sufferings of Paul, but there is no clear indication that the Colossian Christians are facing persecution (though awareness of

Paul's imprisonment could be a warning that they may sometime have to suffer for their faith). The endurance the rest of the letter will speak about is a steady commitment to the gospel that refuses to be shaken or made anxious by any contrary teaching. Since Colossians makes no promises about an imminent end of all things, believers must realize they are probably in it for the long haul and adjust their expectations and emotions accordingly.

Verse 11 ends with the word "joyfully," and verse 12 begins with "giving thanks." The two expressions are probably meant to be taken together. The mood of the passage as a whole is not somber or one of grim determination to wait out the evil or difficulties in life. On the contrary, the ebullient confidence of the writers that God will bestow "all" knowledge and power on the Colossians leads them to instruct the church members to be resolutely joyful and thankful, or more exactly to "give thanks with joy" (AT).

◊ ◊ ◊ ◊

The prayer of thanksgiving and petition in 1:3-11 circles around the idea, obviously appropriate to prayer, that the salvation message concerning Christ and the positive responses to it in Colossae in terms of faith and love are finally the work of God. The growth of "the word of the truth" throughout the world and among the Colossians is a present fact to be celebrated. All that Paul actually prays for is that the Colossians may be given wisdom and strength so that they stand firm in the truth as preached by Epaphras, which means in part that they need to appreciate more what they have already received. This suggests, however, that there is more to that gospel than they presently realize.

Summary of the Gospel (1:12-23)

Introduction to the Hymn (1:12-14)

The section beginning in verse 12 obviously continues the sentence begun in verse 9. Yet there is a change of direction from petition to thanksgiving, and the focus shifts from prayer for the Colossians' future well-being to the work of salvation already accomplished and announced in the gospel message. Whereas verses 9-11 hardly mention Christ (except for the reference to "the Lord" in v. 10) and focus on petitions directed to God the Father, verses 13-14 concentrate on what God has done through Christ, "his beloved Son." This in turn forms a bridge to the Christ-centered affirmations of verses 15-20.

◊ ◊ ◊ ◊

Like Gal 1:4 and 1 Thess 1:9-10, which may also be based on preexisting traditions, this passage summarizes vital components of the gospel in a few words. The sudden shift from "you" (plural) in verse 12 to "us" and "we" in verses 13-14, along with the compressed phraseology and "non-Pauline" terminology has persuaded some scholars that verses 12-14 are based on an early church liturgy, probably one connected with baptism (Käsemann 1964). The shift in personal pronouns has the effect of enhancing the audience's sense that Paul and Timothy share their condition.

The Colossians are enjoined to give thanks to the Father who has made them worthy to share in the "inheritance of the saints in the light." This must refer to the "hope laid up . . . in heaven" according to verse 5, but it is linked or identified with God's already accomplished act of rescuing "us" from the power of darkness and transferring us to the kingdom of his beloved Son. Anyone familiar with Judaism would find in this imagery of deliverance and inheritance allusions to Israel's deliverance from Egypt and entrance into the promised land. The idea of future salvation as an inheritance is prominent in Rom 8:23 and Eph 1:14 as well as Heb 9:15. The language about "a share in the inheritance of the saints in the light" has remarkable parallels in certain Qumran texts that mention the "lot of darkness" or of Belial (1QS 2:5-9; 1QM 1:11-13) as well as the inheritance of "the lot of the saints" (1QS 11:7-8; 1QH 14:13). The metaphor of moving from darkness to light is often used for religious conversion in ancient Jewish and Christian sources (e.g., Eph 5:8; 1 Thess 5:4-5; 1 Pet 2:9; *Joseph and Asenath* 8:9; 15:12), and it has affinities with Plato's famous Allegory of the Cave (*Republic* 7.517-18). The terms for conversion and redemption in Acts 26:18, 23 are particularly close to our passage.

The phrase "his beloved Son" (Gk. *ho huios tēs agapēs autou*) could also be rendered "the son of his love" and may imply both that God loves the Son and also that the Son is a representative or revealer of God's love (cf. 3:12, 14). In the Son believers have redemption, the forgiveness of sins. Their forgiveness is presumably vital to their "being made worthy": it is the work of God in the Son, not the achievement of the members of the church. Yet believers must live lives worthy of Christ as their Lord and King, and for this also they depend on divine gifts (1:9-10). The phrase "the kingdom of his beloved Son" is unique in the Pauline letters, and it seems to designate a realm that is both present and future (cf. "kingdom of God" in 4:11).

Verse 14 proceeds to declare that "we" have redemption in the Son, which is then apparently equated with "the forgiveness of sins." The term "redemption" (Gk. *apolytrōsis*) has sacrificial overtones and is used three times in the undisputed Pauline letters (Rom 3:24; 8:23; 1 Cor 1:30), three times in Ephesians (1:7, 14; 4:30), and in this single passage in Colossians. In Rom 3:24; 1 Cor 1:30; and Eph 1:7 redemption is explicitly linked with the death of Jesus. Colossians 1:20 and 22 apparently use "reconciliation" as a synonym for "redemption," however, and in both verses there is direct reference to Jesus' death. Likewise the author in 2:13-15 will connect God's pardon of trespasses with Jesus' death. We infer that 1:14 also alludes to Jesus' death as the event through which redemption or forgiveness is made available.

The undisputed Pauline letters never use the phrase "the forgiveness of sins," and those letters almost never speak of "sins" in the plural (one exception is in the traditional statement Paul cites in 1 Cor 15:3). On the other hand, we have a comparable expression in Eph 1:7, "[Christ,] in him we have redemption through his blood, the forgiveness of our trespasses." Salvation as centered in forgiveness of sins (though not always connected with Jesus' death) is affirmed in other parts of the New Testament: Matt 26:28; Luke 24:47; Acts 2:38; 5:31; 10:43; 13:38; 26:18; Heb 9:22; 10:18.

◊ ◊ ◊ ◊

This passage offers defining characteristics of the worldwide church in terms of divine action. The church is the community of those qualified for the legacy of saints, already delivered from darkness to a realm of the Son's lordship, already granted redemption through the forgiveness of sins.

Without directly mentioning it, 1:12-14 contains the letter's first reference to the death of Jesus, a topic that will appear at the climax of the "hymn" in 1:15-20, again in 1:22 and, most prominently of all, in 2:12-15. In 1:15-20 the main theme will be Christ in relation to creation and redemption. Colossians does not directly offer a theodicy or claim, with 1 Pet 1:20 (cf. Eph 1:4-7), that Christ's suffering was predestined before the foundation of the world. Yet this passage does suggest that confession of redemption in the Son is the precondition for understanding the ways of God. This is not far from what 1 Cor 1:17–2:2 says about "the wisdom of the cross."

The Christ Hymn (1:15-20)

This passage has long been recognized to have a poetic or hymnlike form that makes it stand out from its context (Cannon 1983, 19-37). Especially since the work of Eduard Norden, scholars have widely agreed that this passage quotes (perhaps with modifications) a self-contained christological statement that probably arose as part of an early church liturgy (Norden 1923, 250-54). Most scholars think that it was written by someone other than the writer of the letter, and some see the writer as misunderstanding or misapplying the "hymn" (e.g., Wedderburn 1993, 39-42, 66-71).

Verses 15-20 in some ways fit the immediate context well and, as we will see, their primary assertions will serve the general purposes of the writer of Colossians very well. Grammatically their clauses are attached to the long sentence of petitionary prayer begun in 1:9. Yet if verses 15-20 were removed, verses 21-23 would follow verse 14 quite smoothly. Verses 15-20 stand out from the surrounding passages by their compressed but comprehensive statements about the Son and their general lack of direct references to humans or believers (apart from the mention of "the church" in verse 18). The pronouns "we" and "you" (plural) are frequent in 1:3-14, and "you" (plural) is stressed in 1:21-23; neither pronoun occurs in 1:15-20.

The "hymn" does not have the formal clarity of some other hymnic passages like Phil 2:6-11 or 1 Tim 3:16, and scholars have differed widely in their analyses of its structure. The following analysis (based in part on Robinson 1957, building on Norden) in terms of two main stanzas or strophes brings out a series of parallels that can hardly be accidental:

Table 1: Parallelism in 1:15-20

ASSERTIONS ABOUT GOD'S SON	FIRST STANZA	SECOND STANZA
who is	15a the image of the invisible God	18b the beginning
he is the first-born	15b of all creation	18c from the dead
he is preeminent	17a He himself is before all things	18d so that he might be preeminent in all things
explanation of his supremacy	16a because (Gk. *hoti*) all things were created in him 16b—things in heaven and on earth 16c things visible and invisible 16d whether thrones or dominions or rulers or powers— 16e everything was created through and for him	19a because *(hoti)* in him all the fullness of God was pleased to dwell
the Son unifies	17b in him all things hold together 18a and he is the head of the body, the church	20a and to reconcile all things through him 20b making peace through the blood of his cross
"everything is related to him"	cf. 16b	20c whether things on earth or in heaven

The symmetry of the two stanzas of the hymn suggests that we should interpret corresponding sections in relation to each other. The six verses of the hymn are built up of short clauses and phrases, more or less balanced in length. The "he is" (Gk. *hos estin*) clauses in verse 15a ("he is the image") and verse 18b ("he is the beginning") seem to divide the passage into two main clusters of assertions. "Firstborn" is applied to Christ in relation to creation (v. 15b) and the Resurrection (v. 18c). Two explanatory "for" (Gk. *hoti*) clauses balance each other in verses 16a and 19a. Verses 15-17 speak of Christ in relation to creation and the continuing existence of the cosmos. In verses 18a to 20 the focus is on redemption (note, however, that formally verse 18a fits best in the first stanza). The statement about creation "for him" in the first stanza (v. 16e) prepares the reader for the eschatological declarations of the second stanza. The expression "and . . . he is before all things" in verse 17a balances the purpose clause in verse 18d, "so that he might come to have first place in everything." "All things in heaven and on earth" in verse 16b is echoed in "all things, whether on earth and in heaven" in verse 20c.

Prepositions ("in," "on," "through," "for," "from") are frequent. The short but powerful term for "all" (Gk. *pas*) appears eight times (at least once in every verse). Inclusiveness is also expressed in the phrase "visible and invisible" in verse 16c as well as in the "whether phrases" of verses 16d and 20c. Nothing is excluded.

Almost certainly verses 15-20 did have a previous life as a hymnlike description of Christ, but the authorship and circumstances of origin will probably always remain obscure. A number of scholars have suggested on grounds of style or content that the writer of Colossians has edited or added to the original hymn. One influential proposal (Käsemann 1964) is that the original hymn lacked "the church" (v. 18a) and "making peace through the blood of his cross" (v. 20b). Theories about the original form of the hymn and the letter writer's changes are inevitably speculative, however, and no consensus has been achieved. We will concentrate on interpreting the passage as it stands in the letter and assume that the writer of the letter expected his readers to take everything in the hymn as reliable rather than attempt to sort out misleading elements and "corrections" (cf. Hartman 1985, 110 n. 5; O'Brien 1982, 35).

The writer of the letter implies that everything in the hymn has Paul's endorsement, indeed that the hymn should be accepted on Paul's authority. Much of the argument in the rest of Colossians seems to build on this hymnic passage. It becomes a kind of "author's assistant" (Pokorný 1991, 74). This in turn suggests that the hymn was previously unknown to (or not well understood and accepted by) the Colossian Christians and the advocates of the false philosophy (2:8).

In what ways is the hymn woven into the texture and thought of Colossians as a whole? The description of the Son as image (1:15a) prepares for the statement about Christians as bearing the image of their creator (3:10-11). The claim that he is head of the church (1:18) is explained further in 2:10, 19. The statement that the Son is preeminent in everything (1:18) prepares the way for similar declarations and warnings in 1:28; 2:3, 6-7, 17, 19; 3:3, 11; 4:1. The assertion about the divine fullness in 1:19 is expanded in 2:9-10. An assumption that Christ's death is the source of salvation links 1:20 with 1:14, 22; 2:11-15; and 3:13. The thought that the church is Christ's body reappears in 1:24 and 2:19. Assertions about dying and rising with Christ (2:12-13, 20; 3:1, 5) clarify the meaning of "firstborn from the dead" (1:18a). The reference to angelic powers in 1:16 is echoed in references to supernatural beings in 2:8, 15, 18, and 20. The universal significance of the Son, stressed throughout 1:15-20, explains why the gospel is proclaimed everywhere (1:6, 23, 27-28; 3:11; 4:3-6). Finally the hymn's positive view of the world as God's creation through the Son warrants the polemic against the false teachers' asceticism in 2:16-23 and the positive teaching about life in the world in 3:5–4:6.

The hymn seems to assume something close to traditional Jewish monotheism coupled with assertions about the Son, which in considerable measure seem modeled on statements hellenistic Jews made about the wisdom (Gk. *sophia*) or word (Gk.

logos) of God. Jewish wisdom literature had for centuries spoken of divine wisdom as something like a distinct being or hypostasis of God, who existed before the world was made and assisted God in its making (Prov 8:22-31; Wis 7–9; cf. Sir 24:3-7). The Wisdom of Solomon speaks of *sophia* as an image (Gk. *eikōn*) of the divine goodness (7:26) and as sharing God's throne (9:4). Philo of Alexandria (a Jewish philosopher and scriptural inter-preter who lived c. 20 BCE to 50 CE) often speaks of both God's wisdom and word (which he seems to equate), though he gives primary attention to the word (Gk. *logos*). One passage offers particularly strong anticipations of statements and terms in 1:15-20:

> anyone who is at present unworthy to be called a Son of God should make haste to submit to the authority of God's *First-born*, the Word [Gk. *logos*], the eldest of the angels (the ruler of the angels, as it were), the one of many names. For he is called "the *beginning*," "the name of God," the Word," "the Man formed according to the *image* [Gk. *eikōn*]," and "he who sees"—that is, Israel. . . . For if we are not yet fit to be considered children of God, we may be children of His invisible *image,* the most holy Word. . . . (*Conf. Ling.* 146-47)

In other passages Philo writes at length about how God created the world through his Word (e.g., *Opif.* 20-25) and how the Word holds the universe together (*Fuga* 112) and serves as its shepherd (*Anim.* 51), guiding it in accord with God's will and guaranteeing its preservation (*Heres* 205-6). For Philo, as for Sirach and the Wisdom of Solomon, the concept of the divine wisdom or word helps explain God's transcendence and imma-nence (God created an orderly world, humans can have access to wisdom so as to grasp the world's rationality and order their own lives in keeping with God's will). All three suggest that the Law of Moses is equivalent to God's wisdom or word, and Philo goes so far as to say that Moses and the Patriarchs (Abraham, Isaac, Jacob) were living personifications of the divine Law. The implication is that the special revelation given Israel through Moses has universal validity.

This is not to say that the hymn in 1:15-20 is wholly based on a hellenistic-Jewish template (Wright 1990, 460). Although Colossians speaks of the "word" of Christ (3:16) and says that all wisdom is to be found in him (2:2-3), Christ is never equated with word or wisdom. Obviously Philo and his predecessors say nothing about the death and resurrection of Jesus, and they do not say everything about creation and cosmology that the hymn says about the Son. Still the similarities are strong enough for us to conclude that the hymn was created by someone thoroughly familiar with hellenistic-Jewish traditions.

Yet, as with the rest of Colossians, in 1:15-20 there is a striking absence of overt references to Israel or the Jewish religion. A number of its individual terms and phrases would make sense to someone acquainted with popular Middle Platonism and Stoicism (cf. Hübner 1997, 57-61). The hymn and the author of Colossians work from Jewish traditions, but do not require their readers to know that background.

First Stanza (1:15-18a): The hymn begins with a relative pronoun (translated as "he" in the NRSV) referring to "[God's] beloved Son" in verse 13. Whereas verse 14 plainly alluded to his death, a subject that will return in verse 20, verse 15 speaks in a present or timeless way of who the Son "is." First of all, he is an image (or the image) of the unseen God (the Greek has no definite article with "image," so the expression does not rule out other images—cf. 2 Cor 4:4). The phrase "the invisible God" indicates divine transcendence, even remoteness, in some contrast to earlier phrases about God as Father (1:2-3, 12). The phrase does not occur in the Septuagint, but the idea that God cannot be seen physically is fundamental to the biblical tradition. This assumption is reinforced by numerous prohibitions against humans making images of God, which is idolatry. Philo often speaks of God as invisible and connects this idea with the thought that the essence of God (as opposed to his existence) surpasses human comprehension (e.g., *Post. Cain* 15; *Conf.*

Ling. 138). Early Christians take God's invisibility for granted (John 1:18; 6:46; Rom 1:20; 1 Tim 1:17; Heb 11:27; *2 Clem.* 20;5; *Ep. Diog.* 7:2).

The chief point of claiming that Christ is an image is to say that he reveals God. The same idea is expressed with other language in John 1:18 and Heb 1:3, and in those passages also the use of present-tense verbs implies that the revelation is ongoing, not limited to the time of Jesus' visible presence on earth. Ancient Mediterranean peoples, especially Egyptians, often spoke of human kings as being images of God (e.g., the Rosetta Stone; Plutarch, *Themistocles* 27).

The meaning here is closely related to Paul's statement in 2 Cor 4:4 about "the light of the gospel of the glory of Christ, who is the image of God" (cf. also Phil 2:6). Christ, as proclaimed by the church, is the key to genuine knowledge of God (1:3-6, 9-10, 25-28; 2:2-3). There is no implication in Colossians that the image is at all inferior to the original. The idea of Christ as divine image also suggests that he brings salvation by causing other persons to bear "the image of [their] creator" (3:10-11, alluding to Gen 1:26-27). Paul in Rom 8:29 and 1 Cor 15:49 speaks of future salvation as involving the conforming of believers to the image of Christ (cf. Philo, *Conf. Ling.* 147 [a passage implying the Word of God *is* inferior to God]). The statement that the Son is the image of God should thus be correlated with the declaration that he is "the beginning" of redemption (1:18*b*): Christ is the first bearer of God's image, and he causes others to share it.

The phrase "firstborn of all creation" also recalls the reference in Rom 8:29 to God's intention that Christ "be the firstborn within a large family." The link between the Son's roles in creation and redemption is also indicated by the phrase "firstborn from the dead" in 1:18*c*. Derivation from a liturgical tradition is suggested by the uses of "firstborn" in Heb 1:6 (of Christ, apparently after his post-death heavenly enthronement) and 12:23 (Christians as belonging to the "assembly of the firstborn"). The term suggests that the Son is "born" *before* any others are created or brought back from the dead, but also that he ranks *above* all others.

"Firstborn" in the Old Testament often refers to the primacy of a family's eldest son, but is sometimes used to identify a beloved favorite child. God says of David "I will make him my firstborn, higher than the kings of the earth" (Ps 88:28 LXX). Israel can be called God's firstborn (Exod 4:22; Jer 31:9; Sir 36:12; *Pss. Sol.* 18:4; 4 Ezra 6:58; *Jub.* 2:20; 19:28). Rabbinic Judaism, partly on the basis of Ps 89:27, sometimes called the Messiah "the firstborn" (*Midr. Exod* 19[81d]); the rabbis also applied the term to Adam, Jacob, the Torah, and Israel (Billerbeck 1926, 257-58). Philo repeatedly calls the Logos the firstborn of God (*Conf. Ling.* 146; *Sacr.* 118-19). A quite remarkable parallel to 1:15*b* is found in the fragmentary Prayer of Joseph (possibly first century CE), where Israel (Jacob) declares "I am the firstborn of every living thing" (Fragment A, in *OTP* 2.703, 713).

Beginning with an explanatory "for" clause, verse 16 moves from the assertion about the Son as firstborn to say that he is the one through whom the world was created (God being understood as the final source of creation). Two passive forms of the verb "to create" (vv. 16*a* and 16*e*) obviously allude to "creation" in verse 15*b*. The world was created "in" (v. 16*a*) as well as "through" and "for" (v. 16*e*) the Son. This use of prepositions to explain cosmological processes probably reflects the direct or indirect influence of hellenistic philosophy (especially Stoicism) as attested in Pseudo-Aristotle, *Mund.* 6 (397b); Seneca, *Epistle* 65.8 (offering a Platonic/Stoic theory of causation); Marcus Aurelius, *Meditations* 4.23.2. For a Jewish appropriation of this use of prepositions, see Philo, *Cher.* 125 (Norden 1923, 240-50, 347-48; Runia 1986, 171-74).

Jewish tradition had previously said that God created the universe through his wisdom (Prov 8:22-31; Wis 7:17-24; 9:9) or word (Philo). However there does not seem to be any direct anticipation of the hymn's statement that God created the world "for" the Son, indicative of a divine eschatological purpose. This is also unprecedented in the undisputed Paulines (Rom 11:36 and 1 Cor 8:6 say that all things are from and "to" God). R. Jochanan (third century CE), however, said the world was created "for the sake of the Messiah" (*b. Sanh.* 98b).

Although the main concern of verse 16 is to affirm the Son's essential role in creation, the hymn seems to interrupt itself in verse 16*b-d* to pile up clauses indicating that "all things" really means everything: heavenly as well as earthly entities, visible and invisible realities, "whether thrones or dominions or rulers or powers." The heavenly and invisible things seem to be about the same as, or at least to include, those clearly supernatural beings listed by title (or category?) in verse 16*d*. While the contrast between visible and invisible suggests a Platonic orientation (e.g., *Phaedo* 79A; *Timaeus* 51A), the string of terms in verse 16*d* recalls and may well derive from Jewish apocalyptic traditions about angelic or other superhuman powers (2 *Enoch* 20:1 [longer recension; *OTP* 1.134] and *T. Levi* 3:8 speak of "thrones" and "authorities" [or "powers"]). Such a catalog is not to be found in Philo, though in one unusual passage he remarks that the air is "filled with living beings, though indeed they must be invisible to us" (*Gig.* 8-16), rather clearly referring to demons and unembodied souls.

The term "thrones" in 1:16*d* does not seem to be used to mean supernatural powers in any other New Testament passage. "Dominions" is used in this sense again only in Eph 1:21. The term meaning a supernatural "ruler" is used again in 2:10 and 15 as well as in Rom 8:38; 1 Cor 15:24; Eph 1:21; 3:10; and 6:12. The term translated "power" occurs alongside "ruler" in all those passages except Rom 8:38. Clearly we are dealing with stereotyped terminology.

The term "power" (Gk. *exousia*) also occurs in 1:13 in the clause "he has rescued us from the *power* of darkness" (emphasis added). In 1:13 and 2:15 the term has the connotation of hostility (toward Christ or humanity), and in both 1:16 and 2:10 emphasis is placed on Christ's superiority to all spiritual rulers and authorities. Obviously, mention of the inferiority of these powers in the hymn supports the polemic in Col 2.

Like the phrase "firstborn of all creation" in verse 15, the statement in verse 17*a* that the Son is "before all things" indicates priority in both time and status. The idea of Christ's preexistence is alluded to in some other hymnlike passages in the

Pauline corpus (2 Cor 8:9; Phil 2:6; 1 Tim 3:16), but it is not confined to such passages (Hamerton-Kelly 1973, 103-96).

The statement that "in him all things hold together" (v. 17*b*) goes beyond creation to declare that the ongoing life of the universe depends on God's Son, who somehow holds everything together. Pseudo-Aristotle *Mund.* 6 (397b) declares that "all things are from God and are held together [same verb form as in Col 1:17*b*] for us by God." Rather similar statements about the universe being held together are made in Sir 43:26 (the word of God) and Wis 1:7 (the Spirit of God). The early Jewish philosopher Aristobulus says that God holds everything together (Frag. 5, in Holladay 1995, 184-85) and Philo sometimes says similar things (*Sacr.* 40). In addition, Philo sometimes calls the Word of God the "bond [Gk. *desmos*] of all existence" that "holds and knits together all the parts, preventing them from being dissolved" (*Fuga* 112; cf. *Heres* 22-23; *Quaes. Exod.* 2.118). Philo's formulations clearly allude to Plato's statement that the will of the creator god provides a bond (Gk. *desmos*) that holds the universe together to preserve it from dissolution (*Timaeus* 41A; cf. Runia 1986, 238-41).

This statement in verse 17*b*, near the end of the first stanza of the hymn, corresponds to the assertion, near the end of the second stanza in verse 20*b*, that the Son's death is the means of cosmic reconciliation. Thus Christ maintains the world's unified existence after creation and is also the agent of its reunification. These statements prepare readers for the appeal for church unity in 3:14, warranted by the declaration that love is "the bond [Gk. *sundesmos*] of perfection" (AT).

The final line (v. 18*a*) of the hymn's first stanza declares "He is the head of the body, the church." The term "church" clearly refers here and in 1:24 not to any local congregation but to the worldwide Christian community. Why is the church mentioned at this point? One might have expected to find here, given the focus on the angelic powers in verse 16 and the general concern of the hymn with supernatural powers, the statement about Christ that actually appears in 2:10, "[he is (Gk. *hos estin*)] the head of every ruler and authority."

A number of scholars have thought that the original hymn at this point spoke about Christ as head of the cosmos, which was viewed as his body, and that the writer of Colossians changed "cosmos" to "church." (This would explain why the statement appears in the first stanza, which otherwise focuses on Christ's relation to the whole creation.) Pagans could speak of Zeus as head of the cosmos (Pseudo-Aristotle *Mund.* 7 [401a]), and Philo says that God appointed his "true Word and Firstborn son" to govern the world (*Anim.* 51; a similar passage in Philo's *Quaes. Exod.* 2.117 is textually uncertain). Philo also says that the relation of Israel to other nations is "as the head above the body," explaining this as indicating not domination but rather that Israel serves as a model or image (Gk. *eikōn*) for the benefit of other peoples (*Praem.* 114). First-century Christians affirmed Christ's lordship over all powers, to be fully realized at the eschaton (end of the world; e.g., Matt 28:18; Rom 8:38-39; 1 Cor 15:25-27; Eph 1:22; Phil 2:10-11; 1 Pet 3:22; Rev 1:5; 12:5), and 1:15-17 has already asserted Christ's dominant position in relation to the cosmos. Still, the notion that the hymn behind 1:15-20 articulated a misunderstanding that identified the universe as Christ's body, which was then "corrected" by the writer of Colossians, is unnecessarily complicated and improbable (Lohse 1971, 55 n. 168).

In the undisputed Paulines the church is called the body of Christ (see Rom 12 and 1 Cor 12), but never is Christ distinguished as the head of the body. Yet that idea is emphatically asserted in Colossians (here and in 2:19) and Ephesians (4:15; 5:23). His lordship in relation to the universe (2:10; Eph 1:22) is now related to his lordship over believers. Christ is presented in 1:15-20 as ruling and sustaining the entire universe, but at present only the church acknowledges his authority as "head." Although the direction of the letter writer's interest after 1:20 will focus chiefly on Christ's relation to the church, this does not repudiate or narrow the claim that he is also mediator of creation and redemption for the cosmos (Dunn 1996, 96).

Second Stanza (1:18b-20): In verse 18 *(b-c)* the Son is called "the beginning" (the Greek term *[archē]* could also be rendered "ruler") and "the firstborn from the dead," implying that Christ's resurrection prepares the way for others, in accord with the Pauline apocalyptic idea of firstfruits (1 Cor 15:20-27). The phraseology obviously parallels the claim that the Son is "first-born of all creation" (v. 15), but now the direction of concern is with redemption conceived as a kind of new creation (cf. 3:10-11; 2 Cor 5:17; Gal 6:15). This already suggests that something went wrong with the first creation.

The application of the title "the beginning" to Christ in verse 18*b* parallels the assertion in verse 15*a* that he is "the image of the invisible God," and this suggests that the term may be primarily an assertion of his relationship with, and likeness to, God the Father. In Revelation Jesus is described as "the firstborn of the dead, and the ruler [Gk. *archōn*] of the kings of the earth" (1:5), as "the beginning [Gk. *archē*] of God's creation" (3:14), and—like God (1:8; 21:6)—as "the Alpha and the Omega, the first and the last, the beginning [Gk. *archē*] and the end" (22:13; cf. 1:17; 2:8). In John 1:1 the statement that the Word was "in the beginning . . . with God" is followed at once by "and the Word was God."

Philo gives the name of "Beginning" to both the Logos (*Conf. Ling.* 146) and divine Wisdom (*Leg. All.* 1.43). On the other hand, he can speak of God as the beginning (Gk. *archē*) and final goal of all things (*Plant.* 77).

Verse 18 ends with a purpose clause "so that he might come to have first place in everything," which reiterates for a last time (in the hymn) the claim that the Son is absolutely preeminent. It obviously alludes to terms for supremacy already employed: "firstborn" (vv. 15*b*, 18*c*); "before all things" (v. 17*a*); "head" (v. 18*a*); and "beginning" (v. 18*b*).

Corresponding to the explanatory "for in him all things in heaven and on earth were created" of verse 16*a*, we have in verse 19 an ontological explanation: "for in him all the fullness of God was pleased to dwell." The best guide to the meaning of "full-ness" (Gk. *plērōma*) in this passage is the statement in 2:9 that "the whole fullness of deity dwells bodily [in Christ]." (The two passages use the same verb meaning "dwell" [Gk. *katoikein*].)

The fullness of God chose to dwell in the Son. Perhaps the phrasing is based on Ps 68:16 (LXX 67:17) ("the mount [Zion] that God desired for his abode") and it may also allude to traditions about Jesus' baptism (cf. Mark 1:10-11). Such an allusion would lend credence to the suggestion of some interpreters that "fullness" in 1:19 is equivalent to "the Spirit of God" (Kehl 1967, 123-24). As the Old Testament speaks of God "dwelling" in the temple on Zion, Colossians speaks of the Godhead "dwelling" in the Son. Unlike later Gnosticism, the hymn makes no distinction between God and the "fullness," nor does it suggest that in his life on earth Jesus departed from the divine "fullness" or "emptied" himself of it (Hegermann 1961, 105-9). Christ is distinguished from God as "image," but he is not represented as inferior; on the contrary, all the plenitude of divine being dwells in him.

The hymn gives its most direct statements on the relationship between the Son and the Father in verses 15a ("he is the image") and 19, and clearly Christ is conceived to have a unique closeness to God. The statement that the divine fullness resides in Christ is not restricted to the earthly life of Jesus (Conzelmann 1965, 139: The writer thinks of the timeless being of Christ, not of stages in a development).

The infinitive "to reconcile" in verse 20a is grammatically in parallel with "to reside," in verse 19, both infinitives completing the sense of "was pleased." God in all God's fullness was pleased to be in and to act through the Son. The formulation is obviously close to that of 2 Cor 5:19, "God was in Christ reconciling the world to himself," although there are some significant differences. The verb for "reconcile" is different; indeed, the one used in 1:20 (Gk. *apokatalassein*) is not found anywhere in earlier Greek literature and may have been coined from the one Paul uses in 2 Cor 5:18-19 and Rom 5:10 (Gk. *katalassein*). "World" (Gk. *kosmos*) in 2 Cor 5:19 (as in John 3:16) seems to refer only to humanity. In 1:20, as in verses 15-17, "all things" ("whether on earth or in heaven") must refer to the entire universe, including humans outside the church, the superhuman beings enumerated in verse 16 and the nonhuman creation generally (Pokorný

1991, 86). When Eph 2:14 speaks of reconciliation through the death of Jesus, the author of that letter thinks of the overcoming of hostility between Jew and Gentile already realized in the Christian community. Colossians emphasizes instead the idea of the entire universe brought back to God. Such a notion of cosmoswide salvation was uncommon in ancient Judaism and paganism, though God's love for all creation is strongly affirmed in Ps 145:8-9; Wis 11:23-26; Sir 18:13; and *b. Meg.* 10b (cf. Philo, *Cher.* 99; *Spec. Leg.* 3.36; *Opif.* 21; cf. *Plato, Timaeus* 29E [Winston 1979, 235]). And Paul did speak of a future fulfillment of salvation with sweeping inclusiveness in Rom 8:18-24; 11:25-36; and 1 Cor 15:20-28.

In verse 13 the writer said that God delivered "us" from the power of darkness and transferred us into the kingdom of his beloved Son—which might suggest a kind of escapist theology that understands salvation as flight into another world. Verse 20, clearly the climax of the hymn, portrays salvation as a reuniting of everything and everyone to God. Grammatically, the statement of 1:20 may mean that all things are reconciled both through and to the Son, but it probably makes more sense to think of God the Father as the ultimate person with whom the world is reconciled. Now the entire world is reaffirmed; redemption is a restoration of an essentially good creation, a healing of its disturbed relationship with its Creator. Now there is no talk of transporting believers from a dark room into another room, one filled with light. There are undeniable tensions in 1:13-14, 1:15-20, and 2:15, at least on the level of metaphors (Wedderburn 1993, 47).

One critical omission in the hymn is that of any explanation of the hostility now overcome through the peacemaking work of God in Christ. In 1:21-22 the reconciliation will be explained in relation to the former alienation and evil deeds of human beings. Colossians 1:20 seems to presuppose that some radical disruption of the world order occurred after creation, a "fall" involving not only human wrongdoing but also the hostility of angelic powers (2:15). Romans 8:19-24 presupposes ideas of a general corruption of the world in line with Jewish apocalypticism

(4 Ezra 7:11-12; 9:19-20; 2 *Apoc. Bar.* 56:5). One scholar thinks that 1:20 presupposes an anxious mind-set widespread among first-century pagans, one of "living in a world that is breaking up, in which the struggle of everything against everything else characterizes the whole of nature" (Schweizer 1982a, 81; cf. Plutarch, *On Isis and Osiris* 45-50 [369A-371E]).

The phrase "the blood of his cross" suggests that Jesus' death is being conceived as a sacrifice, though the text does not make this very clear.

In *Spec. Leg.* 2.192 Philo describes Tishri as the "feast of trumpets" and says that it signifies the ending of wars and thanksgiving to "God, the peace-maker and peacekeeper, Who destroys factions both in cities and in the various parts of the universe." Philo thus has a sense that worship, especially sacrificial worship, symbolizes God's maintenance of the well-being and good order of the cosmos (cf. also *Spec. Leg.* 1.80-81, 96-97), but the Alexandrian philosopher-exegete would surely have been puzzled by the claim that cosmic harmony has been restored through a recent historical event (Hartman 1985). Such hellenistic-Jewish thinkers as Philo and the author of the Wisdom of Solomon generally do not seem to presuppose any radical corruption of nature, certainly not any breakdown in God's created order necessitating special divine intervention (cf. Wis 19:18-22; Philo, *Somn.* 2.250-54).

With verse 20 the hymn reaches its conclusion and climax. The traditional Pauline message of redemption through the death of Christ has received a distinctive universalistic interpretation, for which readers have been prepared by the frequent references to "all" and "all things" in 1:15-18.

◊ ◊ ◊ ◊

The fundamental thrust of the hymn as incorporated into this letter seems one of saying that God decisively revealed himself and acted through the Son, who died and rose again as the individual Jesus but who also existed before creation. The Jewish tradition had long taught that the same God was both creator and redeemer. Hellenistic Judaism sometimes said that the world was created and preserved through God's wisdom or word. The Colossian hymn takes these ideas further by saying that God was fully "in" the Son (v. 19) and that the work of redemption was carried out through Jesus' death (and resurrection). If Jesus is more than a teacher or prophet, is somehow essential to the work of redemption, he must participate in divinity in a way that Jewish monotheism generally regarded as impossible. And, since God is One, if Jesus Christ is essential in the work of redemption, he must be essentially related to creation as well. Something like this logic must undergird the hymn's vast assertions about the Son, which later received artistic interpretation in the paintings of Christ as Cosmocrator in the domes of Greek Orthodox churches (Barclay 1997, 94-95).

This passage goes as far as any in the New Testament in articulating a "high Christology," a view of Jesus that underscores his divinity. It says more than any other about the Son's relation to creation. The Son as mediator of creation and redemption is the chief topic of the hymn, but throughout the passage there is an implication that God the Father acted through the Son. Hence the hymn may be described as both Christocentric and theocentric. The Son does not displace the Father, but nothing is said about the Son's being inferior or subordinate to the Father (in contrast, e.g., to 1 Cor 15:27-28). The hymn further suggests that the Father cannot be rightly known apart from the Son (cf. Matt 11:25-27; John 1:18). A binitarian theology is here attested, one that represents a vital "mutation in Jewish monotheism" and that surely reflects early Christian experience, not least in worship (Hurtado 1988, 121-23).

While thinking and writing in a religiously pluralistic world and without denouncing any other religion or religious community (Jewish or pagan), the writer employs an early church hymn to draw his readers into a foundational confession: that in Jesus humanity and all creation have been given their clearest image of God and, in Jesus' death and resurrection, the basis for universal peace and hope (cf. Beutler 1994).

The church is mentioned in verse 18 as the realm in which

Christ is recognized and currently reigns as "head," but this does not mean that he is Lord only over Christians. Instead, the church is viewed as "the manifestation of a divine operation which is concerned with the whole universe" (Otto Piper, cited with approval in Gibbs 1971, 106). That operation aims at unifying and harmonizing: the universe has always been held together through the Son, and redemption is a kind of reuniting or reconciling made possible by Christ's death.

The hymn emphasizes inclusivism, not exclusivism. It expresses an optimism grounded in contemplation of the apostolic message not unlike the conclusion of a fourteenth-century mystic, "All will be well, and every kind of thing will be well" (Julian of Norwich 1978, 225). Karl Barth in this century argued for universal salvation, partly on the basis of 1:12-20 (Barth 1956, 74, 501-13). While 1:20 does not explicitly promise universal salvation, it does suggest that ultimately no one will be left out (cf. John 12:32; Rom 11:32; Eph 1:10; cf. 1 Tim 2:3-6). Indeed, verse 20 suggests that God somehow achieved this reconciliation already in the death of Jesus. Subsequent passages in Colossians warn of a future divine judgment that even church members face (1:21-23; 3:6; 3:25–4:1). Yet the universalistic hope set forth in 1:20 is never rescinded, and it supports the letter's general tone of confidence and its various declarations that what God revealed and accomplished through Jesus concerns everyone and every aspect of life.

How the Colossians Have Experienced Reconciliation (1:21-23)

Verses 21-23 form one long sentence: Two contrasting independent clauses (vv. 21-22) are linked to a qualifying dependent clause in verse 23 (beginning "provided that you continue"). The basic structure is based on a "once . . . now" contrast typical of early church preaching connected with baptism (Dahl 1976, 33-34). "Once" refers to the period before conversion. A similar pattern of thought will guide the exhortations in 3:5-17. More piling up of near synonyms is present: "estranged" and "hostile" in verse 21, "fleshly body" in verse 22, "holy and blameless" in verse 22, "established and steadfast" in verse 23. The address to "you (plural)" at the beginning of verse 21 connects directly what follows in verses 21-23 with 1:13-20, as though to say: This is how the message summed up in 1:15-20 applies to you.

The statements about reconciliation and death in verse 22 directly point back to verse 20. The reference to "his fleshly body" recalls the use of "body" for the church in verse 18 and points ahead toward a related use in verse 24. The mention of the gospel's being preached "to every creature under heaven" (v. 23) recalls most directly the reference to the worldwide dissemination of "the word of truth" in verses 5-6, but it also resonates with the claims about the Son's relation to "all things" in heaven and on earth in verses 16 and 20.

◊ ◊ ◊ ◊

The passage begins by explaining the meaning of reconciliation from the standpoint of the church, taking the Colossian Christians as examples. They were in their prefaith time "estranged and hostile in mind." The use of "hostile" to describe persons before reconciliation recalls Rom 5:10. The verb expressing estrangement (Gk. *apallotriousthai*) is found in the New Testament only here and in Eph 2:12; 4:18 (Ephesians applies the term only to Gentiles, not Jews, but Colossians does not make this distinction). The expression in verse 21 "hostile in mind, doing evil deeds" may mean an estrangement of the mind that finds expression in outward evil actions, or it could mean that wrongful deeds lead to inward alienation. A similar association of deeds with evil thoughts (using the same Greek term for "mind") is found in Gen 8:21 LXX; cf. Pss 10:3-6, 11, 13; 14:1; cf. Bar 1:22; Josephus, *Ant.* 8.245. Philo tends to locate the foundation of bad conduct in wrong thinking (e.g., *Opif.* 165; *Ebr.* 73; *Sacr.* 2-3; *Somn.* 2.93-109).

The alienation is presumably estrangement from God, though it could also be understood as estrangement from Christ. The undisputed Paulines also emphasize inward sinfulness, though with different terminology (e.g., Rom 8:7). The emphasis on alienation in mind may be designed to make readers appreciate the value of adhering to the convictions enunciated in 1:15-20 and the gravity of mentally withdrawing from Christ, "not holding fast to the head" (2:19).

Verse 22 turns to the "now" of Christian existence: "He has now reconciled [you]." What is the sense of the phrase "in his fleshly body"? It is found in 2:11; Sir 23:17; 1 Enoch 102:5; and 1QpHab 9:2, but not in other Pauline letters. Probably it is used in our passage to distinguish the body that died on the cross from the body that is the church (1:18, 24). Similarly, Eph 2:14 speaks of reconciliation "in his flesh" to distinguish Christ's body on the cross from his body as the church in 2:16.

The goal of this reconciling work was to present "you" (plural) before him (Christ or God) in a condition of sanctity, blamelessness, and irreproachability. This is another reference to the eschatological future, when there will be a final assessment of their "pleasing" of the Lord (1:10; cf. 2 Cor 4:14). The exhortations in 3:5-9 indicate that the readers are not considered to be sinless at present, even though the writer can speak of them as already sanctified (1:2, 12; 3:12) and forgiven (1:14).

That readers are not beyond wrongdoing is indicated also by the careful warning in verse 23: The primary condition of salvation for them is that they stay firmly rooted in the faith and resolutely committed to the hope that they learned about in the gospel (cf. 1:5), which Paul goes on to stress has come not only to the Colossians but to the entire creation under heaven. He does not at this juncture speak about obedience or particular deeds that will keep them on track toward salvation. Rather they are told to keep steadfast in faith and hope. The parenetic section of the letter will make it clear that deeds are important as well as thoughts. Yet, just as 1:21 spoke first about an alienation of the mind, so verse 23 speaks only of faith and hope.

The term "the faith" seems close in sense to the phrase "the hope promised by the gospel that you heard." The faith and hope are based on something outside the Colossians (cf. Eph 1:18). Both phrases point toward a developing sense of right understanding or orthodoxy in relation to the apostolic message—a basis for opposing such false religious positions as the one to be sketched in 2:8, 16-23. The term "faith" in this passage connotes trust and loyalty, but also implies intellectual assent to the truth of the gospel that they have heard, a message given special and authoritative interpretation in 1:12-20.

Why does the writer emphasize here, as in verse 6, that the gospel that is the basis of the Colossians' faith and hope is also proclaimed throughout the world? On a literal geographical level the writer is surely exaggerating (though he stops short of claiming that it is believed everywhere).

The claim is linked with the declarations about the cosmic work of Christ in creation and redemption in 1:15-20: Christ's work has universal effects, and the message about those consequences is being shared with the whole creation (which is not limited to humanity; cf. Rev 5:13—so Lightfoot 1884). The writer may be hinting that the Colossians would be foolish in the extreme if they ever abandoned a message that is bearing fruit everywhere (1:6—cf. Hartman 1995, 39).

The clause that ends this paragraph, "I, Paul, became a servant [Gk. *diakonos*] of this gospel" is firmly linked with the assertion that the gospel has been preached everywhere: Paul himself is the foremost leader in the effort to proclaim Christ to all nations (cf. Rom 11:13; 15:15-21). The phrase "I, Paul" appears in solemn assertions (with transitive verbs) in three passages in the undisputed letters (2 Cor 10:1; Gal 5:2; Phlm 19) and in Eph 3:1, a passage whose content is particularly close to 1:23. The use of the relatively modest title of "servant" (cf. 1:8) provides a transition to the lengthy and not overly modest description of Paul's ministry and authority in relation to the Colossians (1:24–2:5).

◊ ◊ ◊ ◊

This section offers a kind of first stage in the letter writer's interpretation of the hymn of 1:15-20. It directly connects the Colossians (and, by implication, all believers) with the assertion, in verse 20, about reconciliation. The lofty language of theology must, the author implies, be shown to connect with the actual lives of believers, whose conversion experiences should have made them appreciate how distant they once were from God. The Colossians can and must understand themselves not only as persons of faith, love, and hope (1:3-8, 22), but also as persons who formerly hated God and lived accordingly and who still have reason to be wary (1:23).

It is important, however, to note that this paragraph says nothing about the reconciliation of "all things" apart from people already inside the church. It also leaves largely unexplained how 1:15-19 is to be understood. Later passages in the letter will offer some clues.

It is reasonable to assume that the content of verses 21-22 was essentially familiar to the intended readers from the preaching of Epaphras. In verse 23 the writer warns them to continue in the faith and hope they have already heard and accepted.

Paul's Relationship with the Colossians (1:24–2:5)

The passage 1:24–2:5 is a unit distinguished above all by Paul's references to himself and his service on behalf of the gospel and the churches. References to the apostle's rejoicing form an inclusio (1:24; 2:5). Special emphasis is also given to the hiddenness of the revelation now given to believers, a theme linked with the idea that the Colossians need to keep growing in their comprehension of the treasure they possess in Christ.

The passage has its share of redundant expressions of various sorts, such as the use of "sufferings" and "afflictions" in verse 24, "the mystery that has been hidden" and "throughout the ages and generations" in verse 26, the fourfold repetition of the Greek term for "all" (*pas*) in verse 28, the "toil and struggle" and "the energy that he powerfully inspires within me" in verse 29, the "understanding and . . . knowledge" in 2:2, "treasures of wisdom and knowledge" in 2:3, and "morale and the firmness of your faith" in 2:5. Grammatically, 1:24-29 is one long sentence, with dependent clauses attached with relative pronouns, participles, prepositional phrases, and various conjunctions. While not ungrammatical, some expressions in 1:24 and 2:2 appear awkward and likely to evoke misunderstanding. The writer's style is not uniformly polished.

◊ ◊ ◊ ◊

Verse 24 has been a source of disquiet and debate for centuries (Kremer 1956). Although Paul often mentions his sufferings in the undisputed letters, the formulation here is unique. It is noteworthy that Ephesians, although it mentions Paul's sufferings (3:1, 13; 4:1; 6:20), does not link them with a concept of fulfillment such as we find in 1:24.

Here are some of the problems that verse 24 raises, or seems to raise: Does it imply that the apostle is a masochist, enjoying suffering? Does it suggest that Jesus' sufferings were insufficient to bring salvation and that Paul is in the process of making up for ("completing") the inadequacy of Jesus' sufferings? Does verse 24 imply that Paul is the only church member whose suffering is significant? Does it speak of Paul in a way that makes it inconceivable that Paul wrote Colossians?

The context of verse 24 suggests two initial observations. Verses 20 and 22 have already spoken of reconciliation, both cosmic and human, as gained through the death of Jesus. For Paul in verse 24 to claim to be a kind of "co-redeemer" with Jesus would undermine those earlier assertions. For Paul, "completing what is lacking in Christ's afflictions" cannot, then, mean that Jesus' death on the cross was inadequate to bring reconciliation. Second, what follows in 1:25–2:5 says nothing more directly on the topic of Paul's sufferings, but instead highlights his work on behalf of the gospel and the church (1:28-29; 2:1). This suggests, not that the reference to his sufferings is unimportant, but that the suffering is not to be understood apart from his missionary labors. Paul will return to the topic of his imprisonment and its importance for the church in 4:3, 7-9, and 18.

To unravel the meaning of verse 24, we begin by considering the phrase "Christ's afflictions." The term translated "afflictions" (Gk. *thlipseis*) is never applied to the death of Jesus in the

New Testament. Probably, then, Paul's afflictions are not here understood as making up for any insufficiency in Christ's death but rather as sufferings endured for Christ's sake. Or the suffering of Jesus may be thought of as the model for the "cruciform" afflictions of his followers. This would mesh with statements in the undisputed letters that Paul has entered into fellowship with Christ in suffering (Phil 3:10), carries the marks of Jesus on his body (Gal 6:17), and bears the death of Jesus in his body so that the life of Jesus may also be made visible (2 Cor 4:10).

What meaning should be attached to "what is lacking in Christ's afflictions"? Some scholars have detected a reference to the Jewish apocalyptic notion of "Messianic woes" (sufferings predestined by God to accompany the age of the Messiah, perhaps a predetermined quantity of such sufferings—see, e.g., Mark 13:7-9, 13, 19-20; *1 Enoch* 47:2). Despite the notion expressed in the lines following verse 26 of a mystery hidden for ages and now made manifest, this passage as a whole is not dominated by apocalyptic language or concepts (Pokorný 1991, 98-99), and there is no indication that the Colossians are expected to know that rather esoteric doctrine of Messianic sufferings (it is not found anywhere in the undisputed letters or elsewhere in Colossians).

The meaning of 1:24 could simply be that Paul is thinking of the sufferings that he and other Christians will experience in the future—these sufferings are lacking in the sense of being still outstanding. Perhaps the passage suggests such a closeness between Christ and his (universal) church that the sufferings of any or all Christians can be called "the sufferings of Christ" (Yates 1993, 34).

The unusual term for "I am completing" (Gk. *antanaplērō*—found only here in the NT) need not imply that Paul alone suffers or that his suffering is the only suffering that benefits the church. The sense may be rather that Paul is fulfilling *his* share of sufferings for Christ's cause (perhaps there is a hint that God has in advance determined that Paul will undergo a certain amount of sufferings in the course of his apostolic career—cf. Acts 9:16). Additionally the verb suggests that Paul suffers in place of (or on behalf of) Christ or the church (Christ's body), a idea emphasized in the rest of verse 24 (cf. Wedderburn 1993, 38-39).

What specific sufferings Paul has in mind here are not explained, though the readers could readily imagine the physical and psychological suffering that wearing fetters in a Roman jail would involve. Perhaps, however, the writer wishes the reader to think of the wide range of suffering that Paul has encountered in his ministry, such as the experiences detailed in 2 Cor 11:23-30.

In the first part of verse 24 Paul writes "for your sake" and at the end, apparently as a kind of self-correction or clarification, "for the sake of his body, that is, the church." Paul's sufferings are for the church universal; the reason they also benefit the Colossians (who have never met Paul) is that they are part of the universal church. Although Paul in the undisputed letters never says in so many words that his suffering benefits all Christians, he does speak of having a ministry to Gentiles in general (Rom 1:14; 15:16-19).

Paul's sufferings are not vicarious or redemptive, but they do benefit the whole church because all persons who suffer for the cause of Christ build up the church by bearing witness with an integrity attested by suffering. In Phil 1:12-14 Paul says his imprisonment for Christ's sake has encouraged other Christians to speak boldly. Paul's sufferings make his witness credible (Schweizer 1982a, 105). His sufferings do not stand by themselves, and are not accepted masochistically for their own sake. They are the consequence of his missionary efforts for the sake of Christ and believers everywhere (cf. 4:3), and for that reason Paul rejoices in them (cf. Percy 1946, 128-34; Aletti 1993, 136).

The sense of 1:24 may then be paraphrased as follows: Paul finds joy in the midst of his suffering (just as in vv. 11-12 he exhorted the Colossians to "be prepared to endure everything with patience, while joyfully giving thanks") because he knows that through suffering he bears witness to Christ in a way that should benefit all believers, including those he is directly addressing in this letter. This subtracts nothing from the uniquely reconciling power of Jesus' death, but it adds the thought that the suffering of leaders like Paul can be a source of encouragement for others (cf. 4:8). Nowhere in this letter is there an indication that the Colossians themselves are in danger of persecution for their faith, and Paul's sufferings are never presented as a model that they should imitate. Given that in Colossians, in general, only two sufferers are emphasized (Christ and Paul), it may not be too far-fetched to think that in a sense Paul as suffering apostle distinctively represents on earth the exalted Christ who since his resurrection is beyond suffering (Gnilka 1980, 98).

It must be admitted that the phrasing of verse 24 almost invites misunderstanding and could have led readers to draw negative conclusions about Paul. In the undisputed letters Paul speaks often about his sufferings, yet with more circumspection. It is the relative clumsiness of language, rather than implications of vicarious suffering on the part of the apostle, that make this verse a significant though not decisive bit of evidence that Paul did not directly write Colossians. Yet one can imagine that, once the lines were written (by an admiring disciple like Timothy) and read to Paul as he sat in chains, the apostle might have nodded and said, "All right—go on to the next part of the letter." If, however, Colossians was written after Paul's death by a member of a Pauline school, the suggestion in verse 24 that the apostle holds a distinctive or unique position in relation to both suffering and the worldwide church is easier to comprehend; it fits into a pattern of stressing Paul's sufferings also found in the Pastoral Letters (Adams 1979).

In verse 25 Paul calls himself "a servant" (Gk. *diakonos*) of the worldwide church, just as in verse 23 he said he was a servant of the gospel. He further explains his apostolic self-consciousness in terms of a mission (Gk. *oikonomia*) that God gave to him. This mission was "to you" or "for your sake" and it was to make the word of God "fully known." This could be a general reference to Paul's missionary career, as Paul describes it, for example, in Rom 15:15-16, as "the grace given me by God to be a minister of Christ Jesus to the Gentiles." Colossians 4:17 says that Archippus needs to "complete" the service (Gk. *diakonia*) he has received "in the Lord."

In the present context, though, the meaning of Paul's "mission" is probably more specific: Paul's ministry in relation to the Colossians does not include his evangelizing them but rather his general witness to Christ on behalf of the worldwide church *and* the letter he is presently sending to Colossae. So the main sense of this verse seems to be God has willed that the Colossians previously converted by Paul's associate (Ephaphras) should now move forward toward maturity as Christians (v. 28) through the advanced instruction about Christ that Paul's letter provides. It was the intention of God that Paul should write to the Colossians and suffer and labor for them so that the Word of God could be fulfilled or perfected in or toward them. This line of interpretation of "make . . . fully known" confirms the sense of the related term for "complete" (Gk. *antanaplērō*) in verse 24: Paul will fulfill his divinely appointed commission from God, which involves sufferings.

The phrase "the word of God" occurs only here in Colossians, but it plainly refers to the message about salvation in Christ; there are similar expressions in 1:5*a* ("the word of the truth, the gospel"), 3:16 ("the word of Christ"), 4:3 ("a door for the word, that we may declare the mystery of Christ"), and perhaps 4:6 ("your speech"). Colossians does not, however, directly equate Christ with "the word."

In verse 26 this "word" is explained as a mystery that has been concealed from previous ages and generations but is now uncovered. Corresponding partly to the "once . . . now" schema of 1:21-22, the writer indicates that God deliberately concealed the saving truth from peoples of previous times but has now revealed it. Even "now" the message is concealed from everyone except "the saints," that is, Christians (cf. 1:2). The apocalyptic notion of a saving message kept secret until now recalls some ideas and passages in the Jewish apocalyptic tradition. It is not an idea well attested in the Pauline letters, apart from Rom 16:25-26 (which a number of scholars regard as a post-Pauline addition) and Eph 3:4-6, 8-10. First Corinthians 2:6-10 speaks of the secret wisdom of God understood by those with the Spirit but concealed from "the rulers of this age." The general concept might not seem to fit well with ideas that the God of Jesus revealed himself in the Jewish Scriptures (cf. 1 Cor 10:4; Gal 3:8), but the sense could be that God's revelation in those scriptures was not made plain until the coming of Christ (cf. Luke 24:32, 45). The undisputed letters occasionally use the term "mystery," sometimes for special revelations related to the essential apostolic message (Rom 11:25; 1 Cor 13:2; 14:2; 15:51; cf. 2 Thess 2:7) and sometimes to that basic message itself (1 Cor 2:1, 7; 4:1; cf. 1 Tim 3:16). In Colossians the term is regularly used to mean the essential gospel message with the implication that there is something secret or not easily grasped about the message that Paul seeks to communicate (1:26-27; 2:2; 4:3). The Jewish wisdom tradition speaks of the mysteries or unfathomable purposes of God (Wis 2:22), and Daniel speaks of God's hidden designs (2:18-19, 27-28). Philo speaks of the "mysteries" of Moses (*Cher.* 48-49; *Sacr.* 62; *Leg. All.* 3.100; cf. Wis 6:22), by which he often seems to mean esoteric religious-philosophical insights that come through allegorical interpretation of the Scriptures.

Verse 27 says that God deliberately chose to make known "how great among the Gentiles are the riches of the glory of this mystery." The Greek term *ethnē* can mean either "nations" or "Gentiles," and the undisputed letters regularly give it the latter meaning. But the word is used only once in Colossians, and here "non-Jews" makes little sense (Schweizer 1982a, 109; cf. 1 Tim 3:16). Colossians elsewhere emphasizes that in Christ there is no longer "Greek or Jew" and nowhere describes salvation as the incorporation of Gentiles into the heritage of Israel. On the other hand, Colossians shows no interest in suggesting that Jews are excluded from salvation.

The content of the mystery is now identified as "Christ in you (plural), the hope of glory." The message about Christ is essentially the presence of Christ in all who receive and accept the message, a presence in both the church collectively and in every individual Christian (cf. 3:11; Gal 2:20). The writer emphasizes, however, that Christ is present in such a way that "glory" is to be experienced only in the eschatological future (cf. 1:5; 3:3-4).

Verse 28 says "whom *we* proclaim" (emphasis added). The "we" may refer to Paul and Timothy as the writers of the letter, but the switch from "I" in 1:23-25 to "we" in 1:28 and then back to first-person singular in 1:29–2:5 is fairly odd—unless the "we" in verse 28 really means "all of us who preach the gospel." The preaching, however, is now presented as a matter of admonishing and teaching in such a way as to make everyone "perfect" in Christ for a kind of presentation to occur at the eschatological judgment (as in 1:22). The sense is that believers (including the Colossian church members) need to hear and understand the gospel of Jesus in more than an elementary fashion—they need to move on to maturity, and it is the business of the preachers or witnesses to teach with such wisdom that God will judge them to be perfect. The responsibility of preacher-teachers is not discharged when they have initially presented the gospel and won converts—they must also labor to move their flocks toward maturity in Christ in anticipation of God's final assessment (cf. 1 Thess 2:19-20).

Paul is arguing here that when the Colossians finally stand before God he (Paul) expects to be somehow present and to have a part in presenting them to God. If "everyone" in verse 28 literally means all persons (alluding back to the universal salvation announced in 1:20), this text suggests a view of Paul as having an eternal God-assigned role in bearing "mature" witness to the gospel. That shade of meaning is easier to grasp if Colossians is the work of the Pauline school. Perhaps, however, the sense is simply "everyone with whom I come in contact" (including those Paul encounters only through letters).

By speaking of "Christ in you" (v. 27) and the goal of proclamation as presenting "everyone perfect/mature in Christ" (v. 28), the apostle makes it plain that the story of Jesus must be internalized. Just as he had to explain the hymn of 1:15-20 in relation to the sins and alienation of the Colossians in 1:21-23, Paul will go on in chapter 2 to speak of believers dying and rising and so coming to fulfillment in Christ. In chapter 3 he will speak about Christ becoming "all and in all." Paul understands proclamation of the gospel to involve communication of Christ's compelling relevance to the experiences, failures, and hopes of every person, with the result that people discover within themselves and their faith communities not only "fleshly" resistance to God but also divine power working to prepare them for glory.

Verse 29 concludes this paragraph by stressing that Paul labors strenuously at the task defined in verse 28, and he does so with the power God supplies. The apostle takes no credit for the divine energy within him, but he stresses that he works hard by means of it (cf. 1 Cor 15:10-11).

In 2:1 Paul begins a new sentence (vv. 1-3) that, in effect, says, "I desire that you Colossians realize how hard I am working (and have worked) for your sake, as well as for the good of the Laodiceans and other believers who have never met me, so that you and they may be encouraged, united in love, and grow with full understanding of Christ, in whom all divine wisdom is to be found." The term "struggling" (Gk. *agōn*) implies hard and persistent effort, and echoes "struggle" in verse 29. The reference is not so clearly to physical or mental suffering (as in 1:24) as to such efforts as those Paul makes as he seeks to respond, especially in the present letter, to the problems the Colossians are facing. In Gal 4:19 Paul speaks of experiencing pains like a mother in childbirth until Christ is born (or reborn) in the churches he addresses.

In 2 Cor 11:28 Paul speaks at the end of a catalog of sufferings about "my anxiety for all the churches." Colossians 2:1 portrays the apostle as engaged in a contest in a way that will benefit many Christians who do not know Paul personally. As in 1:24-25, 28-29, there is a hint that Paul views himself as having a mission to the entire world, including those he has never met. His active concern for the Colossians and the Laodiceans may be particularly expressed in his letters (see again 4:16), but all the other people who have never met Paul stand to benefit from his efforts.

Before the end of the first century a church leader in Rome could speak of Paul as having taught the whole world, east and west (*1 Clem.* 5:6-7), and 1:28–2:1 may have a similar meaning.

According to 2:2-3 Paul seeks to bring comfort and unity in

love to churches he has mentioned, but above all he seeks to enable them to gain knowledge (cf. 1:9-10). What they especially need to realize is that all knowledge and wisdom are hidden like buried treasure in Christ (v. 3). The idea of treasures of wisdom is widely attested in the Jewish tradition: Prov 2:4; 8:18-21; Wis 7:14; Sir 1:25; Philo (*Fuga* 79; *Heres* 76); *1 Enoch* 41:1-7; 51:1-3; *2 Apoc. Bar.* 44:14; 54:13. Paul does not say that the Colossians shall or should in this life fully understand all this wisdom and knowledge, nor does he claim that he himself understands it totally. What he insists on is that he and they know where that marvelous knowledge is to be found. Perhaps the use of "mystery" to refer to the content of the gospel here, as in 1:26-27, is meant to imply limits to Christian comprehension of the divine truth (cf. Rom 11:33 and 1 Cor 13:8-12). Yet the phrase "assured understanding" seems to place the accent on how much Christians like those in Colossae and Laodicea can comprehend if they look in the right direction.

The expression at the end of verse 2 is remarkable. Literally it reads "the mystery of God, of Christ." Obviously this might suggest that "God" and "Christ" are interchangeable or equivalent terms. Probably this theological difficulty accounts for the alternative wordings of the text in some New Testament manuscripts, with copyists trying to soften or remove the difficulty. Probably the author simply meant that God's mystery also belongs to Christ, or that it consists in Christ (Bockmuehl 1990, 87-88). Yet the wording seems awkward or careless.

The author's preference for an overlapping and repeating method of forming transitions is nicely illustrated in verses 4-5. Here the writer begins to move against the false teaching that threatens the community. Comparable warnings will be expressed in verses 6 and 8 before the main argument begins in verse 9. Yet verses 4-5 also belong with 1:24–2:3, completing the general account of Paul and his right to address the Colossians. "I am saying this. . . ." Everything in 1:24–2:3 seems designed to lead to this climax: The Colossians need to hear and honor Paul's warning, which will run till at least 2:23. On the one hand Paul recognizes and honors their genuine faith in Christ (v. 5*b*).

He is able to "see" that faith, presumably through the report Epaphras has given him concerning the church's condition, but also there may be an allusion here to the power of the Spirit to bring the apostle an in-depth understanding of believers whom he has never met (1:7-8). As he has already said in chapter 1, Paul does not deny the genuineness and strength, the order and stability of the church's commitment to the gospel. Yet he writes now out of serious concern that believers may be led astray through persuasive falsehoods. Faith, however real, is never beyond temptation.

Paul admits the obvious, that he himself is absent "in body," but he insists that he is with them spiritually. A modern speaker using such expressions would normally mean merely that he is thinking favorably about an audience that is geographically distant. Paul probably means more, that in some serious and real sense ("in spirit") he *is* with them as they go about their daily lives and are exposed to the "plausible arguments." Part of the apostle's meaning may be that through the words of this letter, which is to be read probably during a worship service at Colossae (4:16), Paul will actually be present, guarding the church against false alternative messages.

The contrast between physical absence and spiritual presence alludes to the statement in verse 1 about Paul's labors on behalf of those who have not seen his face. The Colossians do not require his personal presence to gain from his efforts. Perhaps there is also an allusion to the false leaders' boasting of special visions (2:18, using the same verb for "seeing"). As Christ is sovereign over all things visible and invisible (1:16) and as the gospel mystery revealed to the saints (1:26) remains nonetheless hidden (2:3), so the apostle insists that he is spiritually keeping company with the Colossians and rejoices in the "morale" and "firmness" of their faith (v. 5).

There is a play on words in verse 4 with the Greek terms for "be led astray" *(paralogizesthai)* and "plausible words" *(pithanologia)*. The false teachers use words and thoughts to seduce their hearers. This is the opposite of the message *(logos)* of God (1:25). Overall the terms already suggest that the

Errorists make statements that are plausible and attractive on the surface, whereas the true apostolic message offers wisdom that is trustworthy but somehow concealed. If the Colossians are capable (as the writer implies they are) of being seduced by falsehood, the fault is not only in the Error but in their own willingness to attend only to appearances. Just as Paul is actually ("in spirit") present despite his physical absence, so the Colossians need to look beneath the surface of things in deciding what to think about Christ and God.

◊ ◊ ◊ ◊

Without becoming very specific, Paul speaks of his sufferings and hard work for the sake of the universal church and the full understanding of the gospel. The gospel is described at length as a message hidden in former times but now revealed with a kind of concealed glory. Running through the passage is the implication that the Colossians need to grow in their understanding of the gospel and that Paul is writing to help them do so. Without a deeper grasp, their faith is in danger of weakening to the point of failing altogether. Since the question of how believers are related to flesh and the body is evidently a basic issue in the conflict over the Colossian "deceitful philosophy" (2:11, 13, 18, 23), we may infer from 1:24 that Paul's labors and suffering provide a model of appropriate Christian self-denial—in contrast to the useless and boastful asceticism of Paul's opponents. Above all, however, this passage (1:24–2:5) presents the apostle as a caring servant of Christ and the church and a trustworthy interpreter of the gospel.

WARNING AGAINST FALSE TEACHINGS AND REGULATIONS (2:6-23)

This passage brings to a conclusion the "doctrinal" part of the letter. There is first of all a summary exhortation to hold fast to Christ and reject the "philosophy and empty deceit" (vv. 6-8).

This exhortation is then grounded by a new positive statement about Christ's saving work, explained especially in relation to baptism and the Colossians (vv. 9-15). Finally the author provides warnings against some regulations (and associated ideas) of the false teaching (vv. 16-23). The pattern of the whole section, therefore, is abAB (positive teaching followed by negative warning, expanded positive teaching followed by expanded negative warning). Grammatically, verse 8 begins a sentence that extends through verse 10. In thought, however, verse 8 summarizes the writer's negative warning corresponding to verses 6-7, whereas verse 9 begins a positive statement extending through verse 15.

The writer seems more interested in making the positive teaching clear than in spelling out details of the position he abhors (probably presuming that his readers don't need full information on that topic). The tri-partite structure of 2:6-23 to a degree parallels that of 1:12-23, where we have introduction, christological hymn, and interpretive application to the Colossians. Here we have an introductory exhortation (2:6-8), a summary of how believers are saved through Christ's death and resurrection (2:9-15), and an application to the Colossians' situation as they confront the false teaching and its demands (2:16-23).

Redundant phrasing continues in this section: "rooted . . . built up . . . established" (v. 7), "empty deceit . . . human tradition . . . elemental spirits of the universe" (v. 8), "circumcised with a . . . circumcision" (v. 11), "grows with a growth" (v. 19), "Do not handle . . . touch" (v. 21), "commands and teachings" (v. 22). There are also some expressions in verses 18 and 23 that seem poorly worded or so allusive as to be almost unintelligible, at least to modern interpreters.

Paul is not directly mentioned in this passage, just as he is not mentioned in 3:1–4:1 (which contains most of the parenetic material in the letter). Yet the writer plainly intends the authority of Paul to back up his vigorous "either-or" approach in assailing the false philosophy.

Much of the driving force of 2:6-23 comes from direct imperatives: "walk in him [Christ]" (v. 6), "[be] rooted . . . built up . . . established . . ." (v. 7), "see to it that no one takes you captive"

(v. 8), "do not let anyone condemn you" (v. 16), "do not let anyone disqualify you" (v. 18). Just as forceful is the rhetorical question in 2:20, "If with Christ you died . . . why do you live as if you still belonged to the world?" The positive and negative injunctions in 2:6-23 obviously build on the exhortation in 2:4, "I am saying this so that no one may deceive you with plausible arguments." However, these stern warnings are supported not only by Paul's personal authority. The writer devotes much of this passage to explaining why clinging to Christ is essential (mainly in 2:9-15) and also explaining why the Error and its regulations must be resisted (especially in vv. 17-20*a*, 22-23). In these short, pointed positive and negative "explanations," which often seem more suggestive than demonstrative, we have this writer's characteristic form of direct argument.

The positive statement about salvation in 2:9-15 is clearly presented as the fundamental basis for rejecting the Error; a right understanding of salvation as thus summarized ought to prompt a rejection of the Error "in advance." The writer seems to be saying to his intended readers: If you truly think through what your baptism means, you will realize why you must reject this "deceitful philosophy" from the start.

Repeated references to dying and rising with Christ in baptism undergird much of the argument (vv. 11-13, 20). Other key terms, images, and ideas appear and reappear as well, contributing to the unity and cumulative persuasiveness of 2:6-23: being rooted and growing (vv. 7, 19); built up in contrast to puffed up (vv. 7, 18); vain (vv. 8, 18, 23); the headship of Christ (vv. 10, 19) in contrast to the mind of the flesh (v. 18); the genuine fullness available through Christ (vv. 9, 10) in contrast to unreal satisfaction (v. 23); the body (Gk. *sōma;* vv. 9, 11, 17 [here the NRSV translates *sōma* as "substance"], 19, 23) and the flesh (vv. 11, 13, 18, 23); putting off or disarming (vv. 11, 15); circumcision and uncircumcision (vv. 11, 13); things not made with hands . . . a handwritten document . . . and prohibitions about touching (vv. 11, 14, 21); superhuman rulers and authorities (vv. 10, 15), angels (v. 18) and the elements (or elemental spirits) of the world (vv. 8, 20); teaching (vv. 7, 22), dogmas/regulations

(vv. 14, 20), human decisions (vv. 18, 23), human-initiated religion (vv. 8, 22); humility (vv. 18, 23); revealing and seeing (vv. 15, 18).

The positive christological assertions are largely structured around the phrases "in him" and "in whom," emphasizing the oneness of believers with Christ (2:9, 10, 11, 12, 15). By contrast, the rules of the Errorists are attacked with "which is" relative clauses identifying these regulations as belonging to the sphere of the unreal: they are mere shadows (v. 17), things doomed to perish (v. 22), futile devices that only seem wise and useful (v. 23).

◊ ◊ ◊ ◊

Introductory Exhortation (2:6-8)

The basic injunction of verses 6-7 is to remain with Christ, to abide (or "walk") in him. "As you therefore have received Christ Jesus the Lord" refers in a general way to the present and past Christian commitment of the recipients, though it connects directly with the reference in verse 5 to their "firmness of your faith in Christ." The Christian faith can be summed up in the confession "Jesus is Lord" (cf. Acts 16:31; Rom 10:9; 1 Cor 12:3; Phil 2:11), and there may be an allusion here to a confession of belief made at the time of baptism. The verb for "received" (Gk. *paralambanein*) is used in a similar way in 1 Cor 15:3; Gal 1:9, 12; Phil 4:9; 1 Thess 2:13; 4:1 (though all of these texts refer to receiving a message, whereas Col 2:6 speaks of receiving Christ).

Paul adds now that this faith must be matched or put into effect by "walking" in Christ Jesus (the NRSV translates the term for "walking" as "continue to live your lives"). The verb in the imperative "walk" (Gk. *peripatein*) is used similarly of the Christian life in 1:10 and 4:5 and, in 3:7, of the life of the Colossians prior to conversion. The whole formulation in 2:6 recalls Gal 5:25, "If we live by the Spirit, let us also walk by the Spirit" (AT). In Col 2:6, as generally in this letter, the Spirit is replaced by Christ, as the power or environment in which believers now exist. Colossians 3 will explain what this "walking" means in terms of inner disposition and outward behavior; in chapter 2 the writer's concern is more immediately with claiming that the acceptance of Christ as Lord is incompatible with worrying about other supernatural powers and adopting the lifestyle demanded by the Errorists.

The thought of remaining in Christ is expanded in verse 7: "rooted" and "built up" in him—which is set in parallel to "established in the faith, just as you were taught." (The metaphors of walking and being rooted clash a little.) At this point the writer's message to the Colossians is not so much "Be what you are!" as it is "Remain where you are!" The sense of verses 6-7 is obviously close to that of 1:23, "Continue securely established and steadfast in the faith, without shifting from the hope promised by the gospel that you heard." The writer should not be seen as calling into doubt his own expressions of confidence in the Colossians' faith (1:4; 2:5). He makes it very clear, however, that the Colossians are facing an enticing message that would from his standpoint—though conceivably not from theirs—mean abandoning faith in Christ.

In both 1:23 and 2:7 "the faith" must refer to a specific Christ-centered religious orientation, such as that indicated in 1:15-20 and 2:6. That is, "faith" here has something of the sense of the content of what Christians are to believe to be true and determinative for their existence. Believers must be grounded ("rooted") in Christ, but also allow themselves to be "built up" in Christ. Christ is the beginning, the middle, and the goal of their existence (1:27-28; 2:9-10, 19; 3:4, 11), just as the cosmos exists in relation to him from first to last (1:15-20). What exactly the writer has in mind in verse 7 by the word "established" (Gk. *bebaiousthai*) is not entirely clear, though uses of the term in other Pauline letters (Rom 15:8; 1 Cor 1:6, 8; 2 Cor 1:21) suggest that the writer is urging the Colossians to recognize ways in which in their own experience God has verified the gospel concerning Jesus.

Verse 7 ends the sentence begun in verse 6 with an exhortation to abound in thanksgiving. Thanksgiving to God is one of the major emphases of this letter (cf. 3:17). In the present context there is an implication that the Colossian Christians should be satisfied with all they have gained through accepting Christ as Lord: They should not look elsewhere.

Verse 8 presents the negative prohibition corresponding to the positive appeal of verses 6-7. No opponent is named. Ancient authors sometimes avoided naming opponents, partly to avoid giving them unnecessary publicity, partly to emphasize issues rather than personalities. Among Paul's letters, however, Colossians is especially notable for the vagueness with which it refers to opponents. The phrasing in verse 8 could leave the reader in some doubt as to the existence of any actual advocates of misleading doctrine in Colossae (cf. Hooker 1973). The specificity of the false rules elaborated in 2:16-23, however, indicates this is not merely a theoretical problem in Colossae.

The term for "take captive" (Gk. *sylagōgein*) is strong and unusual. Literally it suggests kidnapping or taking someone prisoner. It thus prepares readers for the claim in 2:15 that Christ has captured and publicly exposed the hostile powers. So the sense of verse 8 might by anticipation mean, "Don't be captured by enemies [supernatural powers working through human purveyors of false doctrine] whom Christ has already captured!" The warning resembles one in 2 Cor 11:3, though that passage uses other terms, in speaking of the danger of being led astray by a deceitful message or messenger.

The means of capture in 2:8 are "philosophy and empty deceit," an expression that is probably equivalent to "an empty and deceitful philosophy." That is, the writer doesn't here attack all philosophy or rational inquiry (this would hardly agree with his use of philosophical ideas and terms elsewhere, especially in 1:15-20). Rather, he is concerned to condemn a particular philosophy. Later Christian philosophers have probably always regretted that the New Testament's single reference to "philosophy" (cf. the mention of "philosophers" in Acts 17:18) is negative; and some patristic writers were eager to argue that this is no blanket condemnation of philosophy (Clement of Alexandria, *Strom.* 1.11; 6.8; cf. Philo, *Opif.* 77). Philo speaks in the most exalted terms of the true "philosophy" (connected by him with the teachings of Moses—e.g.,*Vita Mos.* 2.212, 216; cf. 4 Macc 5:11, 22; 7:9, 21), but he also denounces certain sophists who claim to practice philosophy but actually only use rhetorical skills to practice rascality (*Post. Cain* 101).

Just as verse 7 piled up terms for the positive alternative (rooted/built up/established), verse 8 piles up others with "according to" phrases, indicating that the "vain philosophy" is based on human tradition, the "elemental spirits of the universe," and not on Christ. Obviously, "human tradition" here has a negative sense and implies a contrast with the gospel as divinely revealed. (A similar use of the term "tradition" [referring to Pharisaic teaching] occurs in Mark 7:8, 13 = Matt 15:3, 6.) It is also clear that "human tradition" in Col 2:8 is connected with "human commands and teachings" in verse 22 (similar phrases are found in Mark 7:7 [= Matt 15:9] as a quotation of Isa 29:13 LXX).

The phrase "the elemental spirits of the universe (world)" is also found in 2:20 and Gal 4:3 (Gal 4:9 evidently calls the same objects or beings "the weak and beggarly elemental spirits"). The term rendered "elemental spirits" (Gk. *stoicheia*) could mean rudimentary things or elemental physical substances. Hellenistic philosophy spoke of four or five such elements (earth, air, fire, water, ether), and some philosophers said the universe consisted simply in combinations of these material elements. Eduard Schweizer thinks the reference is to these material elements, but adds that "it is difficult to draw a clear line between these views and a belief in personal demonic beings" (Schweizer 1988, 468). The interpretation of the *stoicheia* that seems to make most sense in both Galatians and Colossians, however, is the one that regards the term as directly referring to supernatural beings whom the Colossians regard as threatening their salvation, essentially equivalent to the "rulers and authorities" mentioned in 1:16; 2:10, and 15. There is a clear-cut use of *stoicheia* to mean angelic beings connected with the stars or planets in the eighth chapter of the *Testament of Solomon* (a Jewish-Christian document of probably the second or the third century CE). This line of interpretation is also supported by ancient magical papyri, astrological handbooks, and by passages in Philo (*Vita Cont.* 3-4; *Heres* 140; *Spec. Leg.* 2.255) and 2 *Enoch* 16:7; cf. 4:1-2; 19:4 (Arnold 1996, 158-94). In keeping with what was said in 1:15-20, Paul now informs the Colossians that through faith in Christ they have been freed from any need to be anxious about these cosmic beings. The final clause in verse 8 indicates his basic point of attack: The false philosophy is not in accord with Christ. The "deceitful philosophy" apparently took the apostolic message and faith in it as a lower stage of insight by comparison with the higher "knowledge" of the Errorists. Paul responds by insisting that all saving knowledge is to be found in Christ and faith in what God has already accomplished through him (Conzelmann 1965, 143).

Another Summary of the Gospel (2:9-15)

This passage sets out to explain anew what *is* in accord with Christ and Christian convictions. Verse 9 actually continues a sentence that began in verse 8 (and which extends through v. 10). Verse 9 begins with the conjunction "for" and starts to explain anew what being in accord with Christ involves. This passage, like 1:15-20, has some hymnlike features that suggest use of traditional materials (cf. Hoppe 1994, 226-60). In this case, however, the literary structure is less obvious and there are fewer indications of symmetrical formulas or phrases. The passage makes no explicit reference to the entire creation or to "all things." Still, alongside the human beneficiaries of salvation in Christ, some supernatural powers are in view (2:15), and human salvation is closely connected with Christ's relationship to those powers. As in 1:15-20, both Christ and God are the key subjects, though Christ is primarily in view in 2:9-12*a*, whereas God becomes the chief actor in verses 12*b*-15. The jolting switch from "you" (plural) to "us" at the end of verse 13 suggests to some scholars that the writer there begins to quote or paraphrase traditional liturgical materials. The language is compressed and some of the images of salvation in this passage appear to clash (especially those in vv. 14-15), but it is probably more defensible to speak of the appropriation of traditional terms and concepts (especially baptismal ideas of dying and rising) rather than of the quotation of a preexisting text.

As with 1:15-20, some of the time references or associations in 2:9-15 are complex or ambiguous. The statement in verse 9 seems timeless, like "he is the image of the invisible God" (1:15). Verse 10 seems to allude to the entire period after the Colossians became Christians. When we come to verses 11-13, however, we seem to be referred to the time when the Colossians (and other Christians) were baptized or to the time of Christ's death and resurrection (understanding that human salvation was somehow included in those events—as in 1:20). Verses 14-15 focus on the time of Jesus' crucifixion, when the supernatural powers were decisively beaten, though a relationship with Christian baptism is still evident.

◊　◊　◊　◊

Verse 9 defines the relation of Christ to God very much as 1:19 did: The "fullness" (Gk. *plērōma*) of God dwells in him. This is not simply a formula for incarnation since the present tense of "dwells" seems to rule out the idea of limiting this to the time of Jesus' earthly life. On the other hand, the term *bodily* (Gk. *sōmatikos;* found only here in the NT) might mean that the earthly life of Jesus is, after all, especially in view (cf. Goulder 1995, 613). But "bodily" can also mean "in reality" (cf. the translation of *sōma* as "substance" in 2:17), and that meaning seems to fit the present context (cf. Philo, *Heres* 84). An even better line of interpretation, given verse 10, is "for the advantage of, or in reference to, the church, which is Christ's body." Unlike 1:15-20 (which mentions the church only once and otherwise speaks of Christ's relation to God and the whole visible and invisible creation), 2:9-15 refers repeatedly to human beings gaining salvation through Christ.

The plural "you" in verse 10 can hardly refer only to the Colossian church. Rather it must refer to all Christians. They have somehow come to "fullness" in Christ, and this has already happened. The fullness they have realized in Christ must be related to the divine fullness in Christ, which in turn is connected to his status as "head" over "every power and authority." Christ is head of the church (1:18), but also of all the powers of the cosmos. Believers in verse 10 experience the divine fullness evidently because they share in Christ's sovereignty over all powers (cf. Rom 8:38-39; 1 Cor 3:21-23), but also because the energy of God is at work within them to give them new life in Christ. Obviously they have no reason to fear any other superhuman power. Ephesians 1:22-23 provides a kind of commentary on 2:10: God has made Christ "the head over all things for the church, which is his body, the fullness of him who fills all in all."

Despite the references elsewhere to a consummation of salvation yet to come, verse 10 emphasizes that the church and its members have already been filled and fulfilled in Christ. The Colossians apparently do not feel this way—given their interest in the "deceitful philosophy," they must not be entirely satisfied with what they think they have experienced in Christ. Paul insists they have no reason to be discontented, but fears they are in fact unsatisfied or anxious. By implication he is drawing a distinction between appearance and reality, or between felt experience and the truth not only about Christ but about the Colossians. They feel they are missing out on something essential despite their connection with Christ; Paul argues that they are mistaken.

Verses 11-13 set out to explain the fulfillment the Colossians and all other Christians have gained in Christ with the language and symbolism of two rites of initiation, Jewish circumcision and Christian baptism. The preconversion condition of the readers is described as one of existence in "the uncircumcision of your flesh" and as one of being "dead in trespasses" (v. 13). The Colossians in baptism were circumcised with a circumcision made without hands, the circumcision of Christ (v. 11). These former pagans have experienced in Christ a kind of spiritual circumcision, evidently in the event of baptism, a stripping off of the sin-prone flesh (Gk. *sarx*). (As often in the undisputed letters, "flesh" clearly connotes sinfulness in 2:11, 13, 18, 23, although it does not do so in 1:22, 24; 2:1, 3.) It involves not the outward removal of a small amount of physical skin from male converts, but rather the excision of the entire "Old Being" of those who are baptized, females as well as males. This stripping will be explained in 3:9 as a removal of "the Old Being" with its sinful inclinations and deeds. It also symbolizes death, as 2:20 and 3:3 make clear (the same notion is behind the idea of being buried with Christ in baptism, 2:12). The thought seems close to Phil 3:3, a passage that portrays Christians as the true circumcision and comes close to saying that Christians are "spiritual Jews" or members of "the Israel of God" (cf. Gal 6:16). The author of Colossians does not move in that direction, however. His primary idea about the relation between Jews and Christians is set forth in 3:11: "There is no longer Greek and Jew . . . but Christ is all and in all!" Still, 2:11-13 implies that the Colossians know something about Judaism and circumcision.

The idea of inward or spiritual circumcision is well attested in Deut 10:16 and Jer 9:25-26, and it was developed eschatologically at Qumran (1QS 5:5; cf. *Jub.* 1:23). Philo mentions some Jewish allegorists (probably living in or near Alexandria in the first century CE) who did not practice the law about circumcision on the literal level but valued it as a sign of inward purification (*Migr. Abr.* 92). Philo agreed with their allegorical interpretations (see his *Spec. Leg.* 1.8-11), but said they were wrong to give up the physical ritual.

Some exegetes have thought that the Colossian Errorists demanded circumcision, as did the opponents mentioned in the Letter to the Galatians. That is possible, but it is not clearly implied in Colossians; and it would seem likely that the writer of Colossians would have clearly defined his opinion about the physical rite if that *had* been an issue in Colossae.

In verse 12 Christian baptism is interpreted as a symbol of burial and rising again with Christ, which verse 13 equates with being made alive with Christ. All this occurs through faith, and faith is now explained as having for its object God, "who raised [Christ] from the dead." So faith is here, as in 1:4, 23 and 2:5, 7, bound to the Christ-event, though now more explicitly than previously it is oriented to God who acted through Christ (cf. Rom 4:24; 10:9). This is the last of five references to faith (Gk. *pistis*) in Colossians. The unusual expression "faith in the power of God" serves partly as a smooth bridge into making God the subject of the assertions from 2:12*d* through 2:15. Verses 11-12 provide a summary interpretation of salvation as dying and rising with Christ, and they are a foundation not only for 2:13-15 but also for 2:20-23 and 3:1-4.

The general interpretation of faith and baptism recalls Rom 6, with the vital difference that here the resurrection of believers is presented as an already accomplished fact, whereas Rom 6 presents it as future. Ephesians follows the lead of Colossians and adds that believers are already enthroned with Christ in the heavenly regions (Eph 2:5-6). Yet Ephesians and Colossians (especially the latter) do not emphasize present or realized eschatology without also indicating that the salvation will be actualized more fully in the future (Eph 1:10, 14; 2:7; 6:12; Col 1:23; 3:3-4, etc.); and both letters emphatically discourage Christians from "resting on their laurels."

A different idea appears at the end of verse 13, which leads into verses 14-15: Through baptism, faith, and dying and rising with Christ, God has forgiven "us" all our sins (cf. 1:20, 22—those texts, however, link forgiveness only with Jesus' death). The undisputed Pauline letters use "trespasses" quite often in the plural, but never use the verb for forgiveness in this way (cf. 3:13; Eph 4:32). The writer shifts without explanation from plural "you" to "us" in midstream, and speaks only of "us" in verse 14, resuming the address to "you" in verse 16. The shift is abrupt and awkward, but it may well be motivated by a desire on the writer's part to underline that what is said from the middle of verse 13 through verse 15 applies to all Christians, Gentiles and Jews (like Paul) alike. (The formulations in vv. 11-13*b,* emphasizing a symbolic circumcision and a state of sin-laden "uncircumcision of the flesh," fit best the situation of former pagans.)

In verses 14-15 the writer presents a series of assertions concerning Jesus' death, as an elaboration of the claim at the end of verse 13 regarding forgiveness. The writer of Colossians here self-consciously uses a series of decidedly clashing metaphors, though each has a special point. The compressed assertions all pertain to what God accomplished through the death of Jesus: (1) erasing the handwritten text that stood against "us," (2) setting it aside, (3) nailing it to the cross, (4) stripping the rulers and authorities, (5) putting them on public display, and (6) gaining a victory over those rulers and authorities in it (the text or the cross) or in him (Christ).

The remarkable fact is that none of these mythic assertions has a close parallel in the rest of the New Testament, let alone the other Pauline letters. We are reminded of 1 Cor 1–2, where Paul speaks of that death as a revelation of God's apparent weakness and foolishness, which put to shame human strength and wisdom. In that Pauline tradition stand the declarations of 2:14-15, which are the most paradoxical of all this letter's statements.

We may begin with what seems clearest and closest to 1 Cor 2: the idea that in Jesus' death God won a victory. This recalls 1 Cor 2:6-9, which indicates that "the rulers of this age" (probably thought of as supernatural powers hostile to God) brought about the crucifixion of "the Lord of glory," but in doing so they acted in ignorance, failing to recognize the secret and hidden wisdom of God, which God decreed before the ages for the benefit of believers (1 Cor 2:7). The term for winning a victory in 2:15 (Gk. *thriambeuein*) occurs in the New Testament only here and in 2 Cor 2:14, where it describes the divine power at work in Paul's ministry. In Rom 8:37 Christians are said to be "more than conquerors" in the midst of all their sufferings. What is unique in the Pauline corpus is the idea that God won a victory precisely at the moment of Jesus' death (though cf. Eph 2:14-16). Similar ideas are, however, found in John 12:31-32; 16:33; and Rev 5:5, 9; 12:11. Ignatius says that through the *birth* of Jesus all magic was destroyed "and every bond [Gk. *desmos*] vanished" (Ign. *Eph.* 19:3). The "bond" he mentions, like the "record" of 2:14, seems to refer to constraints imposed by supernatural powers.

The powers that are defeated are "led in triumph" by God. The image is evidently that of a victory parade in which prisoners march behind a successful general or emperor (Williamson 1968). The defeated powers are "the rulers and authorities," apparently the same group of supernatural powers designated with this phrase in 1:16 and 2:10. Here, however, they are regarded as enemies of God and Christ. Even though all of these powers were created by God through Christ, at least some are understood to have rebelled and become hostile in a way that must be related to human estrangement (1:21)—even though Colossians never explains how this "fall" occurred (Wilson 1997, 198). In 2:15, however, the divine peacemaking involves not only the violence committed against Jesus in his death but also (and simultaneously) the forceful overthrow by God of those supernatural powers. These supernatural forces seemed to win a battle against God and Christ on Golgotha, but in fact they were the ones defeated. (It is not impossible that this highly symbolic or coded passage implies criticism of the Roman power represented by Pilate and his soldiers—cf. Standhartinger 1999, 214-19, 228). They were "publicly displayed" as defeated foes—but of course only in Christian eyes.

The term *stripped* (Gk. *apekdyesthai*) is often translated "disarmed" (e.g., in the RSV and NRSV), but it clearly is related to the stripping off (Gk. *apekdysis*) of "the body of the flesh" in baptism in 2:11 and the "stripping off" (Gk. *apekdyesthai*) of the "old self" in 3:9. This probably makes most sense as alluding to a ceremonial undressing in connection with Christian baptism. Colossians may presuppose nude baptism (Meeks 1977, 210; cf. Hippolytus, *Apostolic Tradition* 21.3, 20). When Jesus was crucified, his clothes were taken from him (the shame of public nudity was a deliberate part of the punishment). The writer of Colossians perhaps alludes here to Jesus' nakedness on the cross but, if so, his message is that, while the rulers and powers thought they were stripping and exposing Jesus, in actuality they were the ones stripped and exposed as God's defeated captives. In baptism the Colossians and other believers reenact the stripping, literally leaving behind old garments and figuratively stripping away "the body of the flesh" (2:11), their "old self" (3:9). In putting off the old self they are set free from the flesh and from the spiritual rulers and authorities that previously controlled them or tempted them into sinful practices. (Philo can speak of a nonliteral nakedness, which means the soul's release from material things and passions, e.g., in *Leg. All.* 2.53-59.) Thus the supernatural powers were stripped of their power over believers, revealed by God to be conquered through Christ (this idea is developed in the relatively late *Gospel of Nicodemus* 23). God acted through Jesus' death to defeat these powers, but apparently did not destroy them, and at present only faith can discern that they have been decisively conquered.

Returning to verse 14, we see that something has been wiped clean (Gk. *exaleiphein*)—another kind of stripping operation. The same verb appears in Exod 32:33 LXX, referring to persons whose sins lead God to "blot out" their names from his book (similar expressions are found in Ps 68:29 LXX; Rev 3:5; *1 Clem.* 53:4-5). Moses asks that God either forgive the people of Israel their sin (with the golden calf) or else also remove his name from the book of life. It is conceivable that behind 2:14 stands a tradition that Christ petitioned God to forgive his people their sins, like some kind of "new Moses" (cf. Rom 8:34).

In Rev 5 Jesus appears exalted in heaven, and, because of his death, he alone is able to open a scroll with seven seals. The scroll is evidently a blueprint (and determiner) of the world's future. An extraordinary passage (19:34–20:7) in the Valentinian *Gospel of Truth* (dated to about the middle of the second century CE) speaks of "the living book of the living" which Jesus died to gain, thereby bringing salvation to "many." The text continues:

> Since the father of the entirety is invisible—and the entirety derives from him, from whom every way emanated—Jesus appeared, wrapped himself in that document, was nailed to a piece of wood, and published the father's edict upon the cross. O, such a great lesson! Drawing himself down unto death, clothed in

eternal life, having put off the corrupt rags, he put on incorrupt-ibility, a thing that no one can take from him. Having entered upon the empty ways of fear, he escaped the clutches of those who had been stripped naked by forgetfulness, for he was acquaintance and completion, and read out [their] contents . . . and those who would learn, [namely] the living enrolled in the book of the living, learn about themselves, recovering themselves from the father, and returning to him. (Layton 1987, 255)

This passage is arguably referring to Col 2 as well as to Exod 32:31-32, and it brings together images of undressing (and dress-ing) and a book of salvation. (The *Gospel of Truth* contains other apparent allusions to Colossians: 18:11 [Col 1:25], 18:34 and 19:7-8 [Col 1:16]). Yet this *Gospel* speaks, as Colossians does not, of persons who are naked because of forgetfulness, and it presents salvation as a process of gaining deep self-understand-ing, whereas Colossians stresses the saving understanding of God, Christ, and the forgiveness of sins. Another critical differ-ence: The text mentioned in 2:14 is not "the book of the living" but rather a document hostile to humanity, a "record that stood against us with its legal demands."

The expression "he set aside" in 2:14 seems a Greek idiom for total removal or even destruction (cf. 1 Cor 5:2; Epictetus *Discourses* 3.3.15). The phrase "nailing it to the cross" balances "erasing the record that stood against us," and the three actions of erasure, removal, and nailing are evidently facets of the same event, clarifying the meaning of the forgiveness of sins brought about through Jesus' death.

If we read 2:14-15 in the light of Gal 3 or Phil 3, we inevitably think of Jesus' death as involving conflict with the Jewish Law or with the righteousness humans might seek to gain through obey-ing that particular Law. This passage in Colossians, however, seems to go out of its way not to specify the Jewish Law or per-haps to generalize the issue so that Gentile laws or guilt feelings based on Gentile norms of right and wrong are included. Perhaps the term for "record" in 2:14 (Gk. *cheirographon*; literally a "handwritten text") alludes to the idea of a circumcision "made without hands" in 2:11 and thus to the Jewish Law, but the phrasing of verse 14 suggests something more general than the Mosaic legislation. This implies that God forgives real transgressions in the past. In addition, however, Jesus' death either destroys or sets aside as no longer binding on "us" some standard of right and wrong that would otherwise be a basis for condemnation in the present and future. Any law that might condemn believers has been nullified by God in Jesus' death, so that believers are liberated from law as well as flesh (cf. Rom 7:1–8:4).

The term for "record" (Gk. *cheirographon*) is unusual. Plutarch uses it to denote "signatures" collected by ancient loan sharks (*On Not Lending* 829A). Polybius uses the word to speak of a politically incriminating document in one's own handwriting (*History* 30.8.4). The term occurs in the LXX only in Tobit, where it means a handwritten certificate of indebtedness (5:3; 9:5; cf. *T. Job* 11.11). Thus the term suggests a document written by a person who will be held responsible for any failure related to the document. The choice of this word implies that the incriminating document in 2:14 was written not by God (or by any human amanuensis simply taking dictation from God), but rather by the persons "against whom" the document stands (all of "us"). Hence the term suggests not a law imposed by God but rather a promissory note drawn up and signed by humans, who have failed to live up to their own promises. Paul hints that the proponents of the Colossian Error sought to make church members feel guilty or inadequate in relation to special requirements that they themselves had concocted (note the terms *dogmata* ["legal demands"] in 2:14 and *dogmatizein* ["submit to regulations"] in 2:20, as well as the phrase "human commands and teachings" in v. 22). It is possible that our passage alludes to a pagan custom in Asia Minor of setting up cultic pillars *(stelae)* confessing sins of individuals (Carr 1981, 55-58). On the other hand, there are some precedents in the Jewish tradition. In the seventh chapter of the *Apocalypse of Zephaniah* (a Jewish work perhaps dating from the first century

CE), the word *cheirographon* refers to a heavenly scroll with a record of each individual's sins and the judgments to follow (Sappington 1991, 214-20; Arnold 1996, 292-93). A similar heavenly account book listing everyone's misdeeds is mentioned in Dan 7:10; Rev 20:12; *2 Enoch* 19:5; 43; 65:4). But these books are not set aside or "erased." In contrast, the document blotted out in 2:14 appears to be not only a record of transgressions but also a set of requirements related to the demands of the Errorists (2:16-23). God has wiped away not only the record of human violations of the norm of right and wrong; through Jesus' death God has wiped away the norm itself "with its legal demands."

As used in 2:14, the term *cheirographon* emphasizes the humanly invented nature of the requirements/obligations/guilt, and the term thus corresponds to "human tradition" in 2:8 and "human commands and teachings" and "self-imposed piety" in verses 22-23. Although God has forgiven real transgressions (v. 13), what the author stresses in verse 14 is the human invention behind the obligations. Perhaps the writer is thinking of the argument in Rom 7 that, while the Law of Moses is holy, human use of it is not. The writer of Colossians chooses to emphasize the subjective anxiety based on feelings of guilt inculcated by the Colossian philosophy (Walter 1979). Paul's pronounced emphasis on the forgiveness of all sins granted through the death of Jesus here, as in 1:14, 22 (cf. 3:13), suggests that the Colossian philosophy induced great fear that Jesus had not brought full forgiveness. The Errorists stressed judgment and disqualifying of those who resisted their special demands (2:16, 18), and the core of their power over the Colossians may have lain in their ability to make church members feel they were guilty of sins for which Christ brought no pardon (cf. Sumney 1993, 387).

Not only is the "record that stood against us" erased and taken away; it is also "[nailed] to the cross." Here is the apex of paradox. Apparently the writer recalls and desires his readers to recall the sign Pilate put on the cross, "This is Jesus of Nazareth, King of the Jews." It was the charge by which he was pronounced worthy of death. From the vantage point of Christian faith it was false in the sense that it did not justify Jesus' execution; yet it was also true because Jesus as Messiah was the real King of Israel. Also, as Pilate's officer nailed this declaration of Jesus' guilt to the cross, God nailed to the same cross a statement of accusation against believers, a statement that was true in the sense that they were guilty of real trespasses but also a statement no longer valid because God had determined to forgive them.

What is the relation between verse 14 and verse 15? Since both seek to explain the saving power of Jesus' death and the meaning of the divine forgiveness (v. 13), there must be an implication that the supernatural authorities who have been defeated were behind the "record" now set aside. Perhaps the writer thinks along the lines of Gal 3:19, which speaks of angels as mediators of the Law of Moses. One problem with this view is that Colossians never uses the one word that in the Pauline corpus would naturally refer to the Law of Moses (Gk. *nomos*). Possibly there is a hint of the role of Satan or the devil in the biblical tradition as the one who accuses God's people of sin (Job 1:9-11; 2:4-5; Zech 3:1; Rev 12:10; cf. Rom 8:34; *Apoc. Zeph.* 3:8-9; 6:17), even though Colossians never mentions Satan or the devil (in contrast to Rom 16:20; 1 Cor 5:5; 7:5; 2 Cor 2:11; 11:14; 12:7; Eph 4:27; 6:11; 1 Thess 2:18).

In any case the writer of Colossians has set forth the meaning of Jesus' death with innovative ideas and imagery (Lähnemann 1971, 126-34).

Colossians 2:9-15 interprets salvation as the work of God in Christ whereby believers are raised to new life and forgiven all their sins. Essentially in agreement with the hymn in 1:15-20, this passage nevertheless goes beyond it in its assertions about the fullness of saving life that believers have received through Jesus' resurrection, and the completeness of the forgiveness they have gained through his death.

Jesus' death is not viewed as a satisfaction of the requirements of the Father's justice. Instead it is presented as a victory over supernatural beings threatening humanity and as an elimination—not a satisfaction—of demands. Henceforth Christians are to live out the consequences of their forgiveness. Since the fullness of God is in Christ (v. 9), one may also speak here of divine forgiveness gained through divine suffering. The Father wins a victory through violence endured by the Son.

Colossians never speaks of Jesus' death as bringing justification by faith or salvation by grace in contrast to works of the Jewish Law (cf. Rom 3:24-26; Eph 2:5-10), so that believers no longer live under the law (Rom 6:14; 7:4-6; 8:2; Gal 2:21; 3:13, 23-25; 5:18). Yet 2:9-15 seems to echo that concept as developed especially in Galatians and Romans. Jesus' death is represented here as the heart of the gospel because God acted in that death to forgive past transgressions and, further, to liberate people from the possibility of present and future guilt by freeing them from "the record that stood against us." (Ephesians 2:14-16 also interprets Jesus' death as bringing salvation by destroying a law, but specifies that this was the Mosaic Law that formerly divided Jews and Gentiles.) God in Christ has changed the terms of the divine-human relationship. On the human side this entails a faith identification with Christ (2:10; 3:10-11) and living on the basis of the perfection or completeness made possible through divine forgiveness (Weiss 1972, 313). This is not to be understood, however, as living in accord with a new law.

This reinterpretation of salvation through Jesus' death and resurrection is the immediate background for the denunciation of requirements set by the "deceitful philosophy" in 2:16-23.

◊ ◊ ◊ ◊

Direct Assault on the Error and Its Rules (2:16-23)

This passage turns at last to confront the "false philosophy" directly. What is overtly attacked, however, is not a set of doctrines, but rather some regulations for conduct. To support the attack the writer of Colossians adds notes that explain his objections. The passage may be analyzed as follows:

Table 2: The Structure of the Assault (2:16-23)

Reject These Demands	Warrants for Rejecting Them
2:16 Let no one judge you regarding (a) food, (b) drink, (c) feasts, new moons, sabbaths	2:17 these things are a shadow of the things that are coming, but Christ is the reality
2:18 Let no one judge you, insisting on (a) self-abasement, (b) worship of angels, (c) things seen on entering	2:18d-19 these things are empty nonsense, based on flesh-driven thinking, in contrast to holding fast to Christ
2:20-21: Why do you submit to regulations, Do not touch, taste, handle?	2:20, 22-23 you have already died with Christ to the worldly elements—all these regulations pertain to things that perish, are based on human teaching, and are futile efforts to control the flesh

This passage contains echoes of terms and ideas developed in the positive christological assertions of 1:15-20 and 2:9-15. The passage as it stands is rather convoluted, repetitive, and seems to suggest more than explain what the author wishes to say about the Error. Particularly the repetitions in 2:16, 21 and the awkwardness (or obscurity) in the phrasing of verse 23 suggest that the writer of Colossians in this part of the letter loses something of his composure and writes with some degree of agitation. Verses 18 and 23 are among the hardest texts to interpret in the entire New Testament, and the whole passage of verses 16-23 is much less clear than the author's dense but generally lucid positive statements in 1:15-20 and 2:9-15. Part of the reason may be that the passage includes quotations or paraphrases of what the Errorists were saying. Perhaps the style is deliberately obscure, Paul not wishing to explain more than he must of the doctrine or demands he opposes. Presumably he could assume that the

Colossians would understand what he was assailing, even if modern exegetes have trouble coming to any consensus on the subject. A full and neutral account of what he is opposing is not one of his objectives.

The general line of Paul's argument strongly suggests that the Errorists consider themselves to be Christians, but he never explains their ideas about Christology (Francis 1977, 206). It is therefore hard to know what ideas about Christ these false teachers held or promulgated; nevertheless, Paul deals with the regulations on the assumption that—from his perspective—they involve an abandonment of Christ (2:19 may be compared to Gal 5:2-4).

◊ ◊ ◊ ◊

Verses 16 and 18, like verse 8, speak quite indefinitely of opponents: "Do not let anyone condemn you"; "Do not let anyone disqualify you." In verse 20 the writer asks "Why do you live as if you still belonged to the world?" The Greek verb used here to mean "submit to rules" *(dogmatizesthai)* has the same root as the noun employed in verse 14 to refer to "regulations" (Gk. *dogmata*). Since, through Jesus' death, God canceled those regulations and the "record that stood against us," Paul considers it intolerable that the Colossians should now submit to new regulations.

This formulation in verse 20 indicates that the apostle is not just speaking of possibilities: There are real persons troubling the faith of the Colossian congregation. Someone or some persons are drawing a line in the sand and telling church members: If you fail to cross over to our side, you are condemned; if you do cross over to us, you will have to accept a severe new regimen.

These "false teachers" claim an authority to "bind and loose" comparable to the authority Paul himself claims—an authority to define what salvation requires. Paul declines to discuss the troublemakers or their authority. Rather, he attacks the Colossians for being so gullible or yielding in relation to these false teachers. They really ought to know better. Why do they listen to these demands?

In verse 16 Paul mentions judgments passed in relation to "food and drink" on the one hand and "festivals, new moons, or sabbaths" on the other. In verse 21 we hear of prohibitions against touching, tasting, or handling. The "tasting" must refer to judgments about food and drink in verse 16. These judgments could mean the advocates of the false philosophy are criticizing the Colossians either for *not* observing certain dietary and holiday regulations or for observing regulations about food and holidays that the false philosophy opposes. Romans 14 suggests a third possibility: Perhaps some Colossians are practicing restrictions on diet and holy days and others are not—and the Errorists are condemning some or all of the Colossian believers for not considering such matters essential. Colossians 2:16 does not make clear what kinds of judgments are in view.

Scholars have often detected a Jewish flavor in the false philosophy, especially because of the reference to "sabbaths and new moons," but also because of the food restrictions (a rather close parallel to the terminology of verse 20 is found in the *Letter of Aristeas* 142). Yet especially the prohibitions against touching or tasting (v. 21) seem to go well beyond ordinary Jewish food restrictions (DeMaris 1994, 58). Ancient pagans as well as Jews often observed dietary rules and fasting, sometimes to prepare for visionary experiences or to ward off evil powers (Arnold 1996, 210-12; Lesses 1998). Thus Epictetus asks "Is it possible at the present time that all the opinions which Jews and Syrians and Egyptians and Romans hold on the subject of food are correct?" (*Discourses* 1.11.12). Dietary discipline was also a significant part of some philosophical traditions, notably Pythagoreanism and Middle Platonism, as evidenced for example in Timaeus Locrus's *On the Nature of the World and the Soul*, and it was linked with teaching about restraining wrongful desire, as in 2:23 (DeMaris 1994, 109-12). Judaism and Middle Platonism were combined in Philo of Alexandria, and he gives a detailed description of a Jewish monastic community, that of the Therapeutae, where men and women observed a celibate lifestyle and a simple meat-free diet, being devoted to the study of the Mosaic scriptures and philosophy (*Vita Cont.* 67-74). Philo says the Therapeutae fasted and maintained a plain diet to preclude self-indulgence (*Vita Cont.* 34-37, 67-74; *Vita Cont.* 37 and Col 2:23 use the same Greek term for "self-indulgence"). On the other hand, Philo and the Therapeutae did not advocate worship of angels (either in the sense of worshiping angels or worshiping God in company with angels), and the Torah-centeredness of Philo and the Therapeutae is not clearly paralleled by any comparable devotion to the Jewish Law on the part of the Colossian Errorists.

As for the term "sabbaths," that very likely does refer to the fundamental Jewish holy day. It could conceivably refer to a Christian sabbath, however. One recent interpreter argues that 2:16 refers to Christian observances of festivals, new moons, and sabbaths—and that the "deceitful philosophy" was a Cynic position critical of all religious calendars (Martin 1996, 124-34). Given the vagueness of the wording in verse 18, this line of interpretation is a slender but real possibility.

"New moons" may well refer to Jewish festivals, but there were pagan lunar festivals as well, especially ones connected with Artemis and Men, deities known to have been worshiped in the environs of Colossae (see Arnold 1996, 216). The phraseology of verse 16 recalls God's words in Isa 1:13-14 LXX, "I cannot bear your new moons and sabbaths, and the great day, your fasting . . . my soul hates." Yet the parallel is not so close that we must assume that Paul has this Old Testament passage in mind, or expects the readers to recall it (for the combination of terms, see further 1 Chron 23:31; 2 Chron 2:4; 31:3; Ezek 45:17; Hos 2:11; cf. *Jub.* 1:14). Perhaps it is significant that Philo interpreted the sabbath as a day of rest for the body so that the soul might pursue (Mosaic) philosophy (*Spec. Leg.* 2.61) and the feast of the new moon as symbolizing the value of giving generously to deserving persons and controlling primitive appetites with reason (*Spec. Leg.* 2.141-42). Thus Philo interprets circumcision and these particular holy days as symbols of spiritual mastery of the physical life with its passions. Perhaps the "false teachers" also advocated observance of rites and festivals on the ground that they promoted victory over the flesh (cf. 2:23).

In verse 17 Paul says these things (judgments about food, drink, or festivals) are a "shadow [Gk. *skia*] of what is to come, but the substance [Gk. *sōma*] belongs to Christ." This suggests that the Errorists teach only about physical matters, things that for Paul (as for Plato) are symbols of the true immaterial realities (which Paul identifies as things "to come"). Philo occasionally uses *skia* and *sōma* in this shadow/reality sense (e.g., *Conf. Ling.* 190; *Migr. Abr.* 12). The phrase "shadow of what is to come" in 2:17 implies a non-Philonic futuristic eschatology that the author of Colossians refuses to abandon or neglect, however much he also wants to stress that believers have found the fullness of salvation already in Christ.

The term "shadow" may here suggest that the Error contains relative truth and value. Hebrews 10:1 characterizes the Old Testament ordinances about priesthood and sacrifice as a "shadow," interpreting them as a true but now obsolete revelation that points to the perfect sacrifice of Christ. Perhaps 2:17 concedes that the Error points in the direction of the truth, while falling short of the reality that belongs to Christ (v. 23 can be read as implying that the goal of self-control is valid, though the Error's ascetic path does not achieve it).

In verse 18 Paul says, "Do not let anyone disqualify you" (like an umpire). The Greek term for "disqualify" is quite unusual, but the warning seems essentially parallel to "do not let anyone condemn you" in verse 16.

This false teacher and judge insists on humility. "Humility" will be cited again in verse 23 as one of the essential emphases of the false teaching, and in 3:12 Paul will praise it as an indispensable Christian virtue (cf. Eph 4:2; Phil 2:3). In 2:18 this humble orientation is linked, evidently, with "worship of angels." Perhaps the sense is that the false philosophy urges the Colossians to show humility or deference toward angels, or perhaps the term refers to fasting or other particular devotional disciplines, as in *Herm. Vis.* 3.10.6.

But what specifically is this "worship of angels"? Is it human worship directed toward angels, as scholars before Fred Francis generally assumed? Or is it worship of God in which humans somehow participate jointly alongside angels, as Francis argued especially on the basis of parallels in Jewish apocalyptic texts? The Letter to the Hebrews speaks of Christians on earth joining now in the worship of the heavenly Jerusalem, in company with "innumerable angels in festal gathering" (12:22), and that letter begins with a kind of liturgy summoning angels to worship and serve Christ as God's Son (1:6). Jewish apocalyptic texts often make connections between human and angelic worship (Francis 1975a). The Qumran text *Songs of the Sabbath Sacrifice* is a particularly important text in the Jewish tradition of seeing (valid) worship of God as performed in communion with angelic worshipers (Newsom 1985, 17-72). So 2:18 *may* refer to human beings joining with angels in worship of God. But why would the author of Colossians object to such monotheistic worship? Francis thinks the problem is that it encouraged a species of Christian elitism: Only a few special persons of "vision" could participate (Francis 1977, 204-5). Yet Paul does not criticize the Errorists for fostering elitism.

On the other hand, it is easy to see why worship directed toward angels would offend mainstream Jews and Christians—and Paul. The book of Revelation warns a prophet not to worship angels (19:10; 22:8-9), and this warning is probably based on a Jewish tradition opposed to such worship and expressed in *Apoc. Zeph.* 6:14-15. Papias, a second-century bishop of Hierapolis, speaks about angels, perhaps warning against giving them undue reverence. Canon 35 of the Council of Laodicea (fourth century CE) forbids the worship of angels. Origen reports the pagan accusation that Jews worship heaven and the angels in it (*C. Celsum* 5.6). No other known passage in ancient literature uses the term translated in 2:18 as "worship" (Gk. *thrēskeia*) together with a phrase in the genitive case (like the one translated "of angels" in this verse) in such a way that the latter refers to superhuman worshipers. On the other hand, *thrēskeia* is often found with genitive expressions indicating the object of worship (Arnold 1996, 91-93).

Are the angels mentioned in 2:18 more or less the same beings called "rulers and authorities" in 2:10 and 15? If they are among the foes defeated by God in Jesus' death, the "worship of angels" in verse 18 can hardly be considered benign. Or perhaps the angels mentioned in verse 18 were worshiped or venerated with the understanding that they would guard the human worshipers against the threats of other supernatural powers (the dangerous "rulers and authorities"). Perhaps the "worship" mentioned in verse 18 did not involve a deliberate downgrading of Christ or God in favor of giving exclusive devotion to angels; it may have involved, rather, the venerating of angels as potent mediators, able to extend special help or protection, rather in line with folk magic (Arnold 1996, 101-2). Possibly the phrase "worship of angels" was not a term the Errorists themselves employed but was one coined by Paul in order to dramatically express his judgment that the erroneous teaching would draw the Colossians away from the true worship of God through Christ.

The next clause in verse 18 is the most baffling of all, and might be literally translated "which things he [someone] has seen while entering." Does the "which things" refer back to "self-abasement" and "worship of angels" and does the "entering" imply entrance into heaven (a heavenly vision)? Another possible translation is "he enters on the things that he has previously seen" (meaning that he steps into a realm or world he has previously seen in a vision). The RSV translates the clause "taking his stand on visions." The REB has "people who go in for self-mortification and angel-worship and access to some visionary world." The NRSV translates the clause "dwelling on visions," but a footnote adds that the meaning of the Greek text is uncertain! The presumption of this last translation seems to be that the advocate of mortification and worship of angels defends this advocacy by citing visions (cf. Stuckenbruck 1995, 117-19).

If the proponents of the "deceitful philosophy" are Jewish, they represent a Judaism emphasizing mystical experiences and visions as the basis for authority (rather than the Law of Moses); and their position seems to incorporate pagan traditions. But the proponents are not necessarily Jewish. It is quite possible that the choice of the unusual term for "entering" (Gk. *embateuein*) is at least a metaphorical reference to pagan mystery initiations and visionary experiences linked with them. A fragmentary text attributed to Posidonius, a Stoic philosopher of the first century BCE, uses the term in celebrating human greatness: man "crosses the seas, he *enters into* heaven in contemplation" (Theiler 1982, Fragment 309A, line 63). Perhaps the Error had some of the features of an astral religion (Hartman 1995, 29-32).

In the last part of verse 18 Paul gives his own opinion of the person claiming those visions: "He is really functioning on the basis of his flesh-governed mind!" (AT). This kind of ad hominem attack might be called ancient psychological criticism. The charge is that the Errorists claim to have special spiritual experiences—whereas in fact all they are reporting are projections of their sin-dominated minds. Verse 23 launches another kind of psychological attack: The Error aims at controlling the flesh (something Paul apparently applauds), but in fact these regulations and doctrines fail to achieve that goal. Perhaps Paul alludes to the behavior of the Errorists, or perhaps he is appealing to general human experience (to the effect that trying to apply such rules as these Errorists commend does not free the mind of tempting thoughts). This mode of psychological criticism is related to Paul's repeated assertion that the Error is a product of human invention rather than divine revelation. The "false teacher" thinks (or at least claims) that he has seen extraordinary visions of heavenly things (like Paul in 2 Cor 12:1-4); in fact, however, he is only imagining that fantasies of his fleshly mind represent objective reality. The Greek term *physioumenos* means "puffed up," implying arrogance as well as error; and it involves a sardonic comment on the Errorist's claims to follow a path of humility.

The primary criticism is given, however, in verse 19: The Errorists fail to hold fast to Christ, who, as head, is the means of nourishment for the entire body of the church (God being the ultimate source of growth). If the whole cosmos exists and is held together only through Christ (1:17), reliance on Christ for growth and cohesion should be the most obvious thing in the world to members of Christ's body. Only in Christ can they live, only through staying connected with him can they remain spiritually alive. Perhaps verse 19 implies that the Errorists were trying to outgrow ordinary Christianity or even outgrow their need of Christ. Again, the essential criticism of the Error is christological: that it means a break with Christ (the writer doesn't say that the Errorists were conscious of this—only that that was the objective result of their teaching). The phrase "ligaments and sinews" in verse 19 contributes to the liveliness of the image; but it does not seem to refer to any particular leaders or structures in the church—all of the church's health and strength comes from its staying bound with God through Christ. The Errorists pretend to "grow" by self-puffery, or the "hot air" of the flesh; the true Body of Christ grows by staying connected to God.

Ephesians 4:13-16, obviously dependent on Col 2:19, connects growth in the church with a commitment to love and truth, in contrast to false doctrines and deceitful teachers. Ephesians speaks of Christ's present superiority to all supernatural powers, though some of them still threaten his followers (1:22-23; 6:12-18). Significantly, the author of Ephesians does not use or explain such obscure phrases as "the elemental spirits of the universe" "worship of angels," and "dwelling on visions." Possibly already in his day these terms had become enigmatic.

Almost as though starting over again in his critique, Paul asks in verse 20, "If with Christ you died to the elemental spirits of the universe, why do you live as if you still belonged to the universe?" This comes closer than verses 16-19 to referring directly to the soteriological claims of 2:9-15: Christians have already died (and risen) with Christ. With Christ they have been cut off from the realm of the flesh or the world. But how is the triumph of God in Jesus' death over the hostile powers in verse 15 meaningful for this polemic? It is most obviously meaningful if the "elemental spirits of the universe" (2:8, 20) are closely related to, or identical with, the "rulers and authorities" who were defeated in the cross. Believers are set free from the domination or the fear of such powers. Why then do they submit to the regulations of the false teachers, which recall the "legal demands" of the "record" that God set aside when Jesus was crucified? Somehow the supernatural powers stood behind the regulations that were set aside by God, and believers in Christ have been liberated by his death from the power of those regulations, those supernatural powers, and "the body of flesh." The terminology of the passage is obscure, but some such reading of the whole train of thought in 2:9-23 seems to give the passage more coherence than any other—even though many of the details of the erroneous teaching remain obscure.

Perhaps the Error dealt more with concepts of salvation and who received it than directly with beliefs about Christ (Francis 1977, 206). Perhaps the Errorists talked mainly about what believers still needed to do by way of keeping certain special rules and seeking certain spiritual ecstasies. Perhaps they encouraged a radical individualism rather than community responsibilities (Van Broekhoven 1997, 89). Still, the writer of Colossians (our only source of information about the Error) insists that the basic problem *was* Christology—regardless of how the Errorists saw things. The basic failure of the Errorists was that they saw limitations in the "saving work" of Christ—and they tried to make up what was lacking (cf. 1:24) through their own specially constructed disciplines. Christian soteriology is, first of all, an understanding of what Christ does in relation to human salvation; the Errorists' view was that, whatever Christ accomplished, it was not enough. Paul's rhetoric has a strong binary "either-or" implication: If you are with Christ, you must not submit to forces and regulations of "the world."

"Why do you live as if you still belonged to the world?" demands Paul in verse 20*b*. He then goes on with examples of the regulations that the Errorists were trying to impose in Colossae: "Do not handle, Do not taste, Do not touch." The prohibition of tasting seems to repeat the idea of verse 16 about judgments regarding food and drink; now the sense is clear that some things are to be entirely avoided. But the verbs in verse 21 have no objects, and we can only guess what things the Errorists have in mind. A number of exegetes have supposed that the rule against touching prohibits sexual activity (cf. 1 Cor 7:1: "It is well for a man not to touch a woman"). It is certainly conceivable that sexual renunciation was demanded as a spiritual discipline or prerequisite for visionary experiences (cf. Exod 19:15 and, e.g., Philo's *Vita Mos.* 2.68). However, Paul's dismissal of these matters as "things that perish with use" (v. 22*a*) makes it hard to think that sexual activity is under consideration (in 1 Cor 6:12-20 food issues are viewed as spiritually neutral, but sexual ones are not). Colossians 2:22*b* further describes the Errorists' rules as based on "human commands and teachings." This phrase repeats almost exactly a phrase in Isa 29:13 LXX, which is explicitly cited in the gospel story about defilement (Matt 15:9 = Mark 7:7). The writer of Colossians may intend to allude to the Old Testament text, but it is also possible that he expects his readers to recall that gospel story dealing with food and false notions of purity. Corresponding to the remark about the "human way of thinking" of the false leader in verse 18, verse 23 goes on to say that the prohibitions and teachings have the surface appearance of "wisdom" (cf. the allusions to the divine word and wisdom in 1:15-20). This appearance of wisdom is marked by a "self-imposed piety, [and] humility" (cf. the phrase "self-abasement and worship of angels" in v. 18). It is further marked by "severe treatment of the body"—that is, an appearance of impressive self-control.

The term "self-imposed piety" (the Greek term is used only here in the New Testament, and not attested anywhere prior to Colossians) might also mean "self-made religion" (Bauer 1979, 218). The term fits with "human commands and teachings" (v. 22*b*) and suggests that the entire religious position of the Errorists is a humanly constructed pseudo-religion. The Greek term ends in "-*skia*," which suggests a punning allusion to the charge in verse 17 that the Error's regulations are mere "shadow" or "illusion" (Gk. *skia*).

The final clause in verse 23 is virtually impenetrable. Literally it runs "not in some honor for the indulgence of the flesh." Perhaps the general sense is that the regulations of the Errorists, while apparently promoting genuine devotion and restraint of fleshly appetites, actually are of no benefit and somehow foster self-indulgence, not restraint. The term for "indulgence" could also be translated "fulfillment," and there may be here an ironic allusion to Paul's claim that true fulfillment is to be found in Christ (and only in him—2:9-10): The only fulfillment the Errorists inculcate is "fleshly"!

Perhaps the closest parallel to the Colossian Error thus far identified is to be found in a Nag Hammadi document, tractate *Zostrianos* (NHC VIII, 1), a work that may be dated as early as the beginning of the third century CE. The tractate recounts the heavenly journey of a visionary who turned away from the body, experienced a series of baptisms connected with various angelic beings, and finally became an angel himself. His spiritual transformation is portrayed with Middle Platonic philosophical concepts. At the end the visionary returns to the ordinary world to preach to elect members of "the race of Seth"; he warns them not to "baptize yourselves with death nor entrust yourselves to those who are inferior to you" (131, 2-5) and he advocates celibacy, urging them to "flee from the madness and the bondage of femaleness, and choose for yourselves the salvation of maleness." Harold Attridge thinks the Nag Hammadi document opposed a Pauline interpretation of baptism as dying with Christ (such as that in 2:9-15) and proclaimed a kind of "worship of angels" in that human beings became angel-like, rejected marriage (Mark 12:25 parallels), and claimed to arrive at a kind of heavenly "wisdom" closely related to Platonism. This may not be "Gnosticism" in a full-blown sense, but the Colossian Error probably arose "in the context of a community that sought after visionary experience and tried to prepare for it ritually" (Attridge 1994, 497). The tractate's ideas may have roots in Jewish apocalyptic literature (especially *1–3 Enoch*) and in hellenistic Judaism (Attridge cites Philo of Alexandria's description of the Therapeutae). The dating of the ideas presented in the tractate and the document's relation to Christianity are very uncertain. Still, *Zostrianos* does illustrate how the critique in Colossians might refer to a fairly coherent syncretistic movement that mixed pagan, Jewish, apocalyptic, and philosophical ingredients.

◊   ◊   ◊   ◊

While Paul does not give a full or perfectly lucid account of the false philosophy, he does provide a clear and consistent rationale for rejecting it. His fundamental objection is that it does not focus on Christ, whereas the church's contact with reality and relationship with God depend on staying firmly connected with him. Paul's fundamental assurance to the Colossians is that Christ (or God through Christ) has always been superior to all "dominions or rulers" (1:16) and in the cross has already defeated all hostile "rulers and authorities" (2:15; cf. 1:20), thereby making all Christians superior to any threat that the supernatural powers (somehow honored by the Errorists) might seem to pose. The false philosophy concentrates on making up rules to control fleshly desires, but this approach is futile. It is based on human traditions, human-invented religion or, perhaps, a religion invented by angels for human use, rather than one revealed by God. True worship, for Paul, consists of giving thanks to God through Christ in everything (3:17), a worship implied already in the Christ hymn of 1:15-20.

It seems altogether possible that the teachers of the false philosophy did not think of themselves—or present themselves in Colossae—as teaching abandonment of Christ; they may well have said that they only sought to make salvation more certain by means of hidden knowledge and special ritual and moral practices. This was, in effect, to tell the Colossians that Christ and faith in him were uncertain or insufficient without the distinctive "good works" defined by this "philosophy." From the viewpoint of the author of Colossians, the teachers who thus claimed to improve on "Christ alone" led their disciples into a catastrophic "aloneness without Christ." And, since the fullness of God is to be found in Christ, this also meant a catastrophic separation from God. From Paul's perspective, lemmings who followed these pied pipers into new religious adventures might master strenuous spiritual disciplines and have ecstatic visions, but at the end of the day they would drop off a cliff.

Paul urges the Colossians to show no tolerance for this "deceitful philosophy." Believers must choose an exclusive loyalty to Christ, and this means resisting any anxieties about the lingering power of the "principalities and powers" and any inclination to feel guilty in regard to the special ritual and moral regulations advocated by the Errorists. Yet Paul's expressions of intolerance toward the Error are not accompanied by anathemas for the false teachers, in contrast to the approach taken in Gal 1:8-9; 5:10. This suggests a hope for ultimate reconciliation, just as 2:14-15 read together with 1:20 implies that the supernatural beings hostile to God are defeated but not annihilated.

PARENETIC SECTION: EXHORTATIONS FOR THE NEW LIFE (3:1–4:6)

This section presents the letter's primary teaching about how believers should live. The two main sections of the letter are thus a theological exposition (with polemic) in 1:13–2:23 and this hortatory one. Similar divisions into doctrinal and parenetic sections are found in other Pauline letters (Rom 1:18–11:32 + 12:1–15:13; Gal 1:6–5:12 + 5:13–6:10; Eph 1:3–3:21 + 4:1–6:20). Within the parenetic material there are four major subsections: an introduction (3:1-4), a series of instructions for all Christians about vices to "put off" and virtues to "put on" (3:5-17), a "household code" describing duties for different groups (wives-husbands, children-parents, slaves-masters) within the church (3:18–4:1), and a concluding section emphasizing duties toward outsiders (4:2-6).

The entire passage lacks specific references to the situation of the Colossians—although the delineation of the Christian way of life presents a positive alternative to the regulations of the Errorists attacked in chapter 2. Grammatically, most of the passage consists of direct instructions (using verbs in the imperative mood or participles with imperatival force). The instructions are frequently supported by concise warrants expressed in the indicative (3:3-4, 6, 9b-11, 13c, 14b, 15b, 24-25; 4:1b). The smooth flow of pithy injunctions without lengthy argument suggests that the author here is largely presenting material that he or some other Christian writer(s) had previously shaped and polished—possibly in connection with baptismal liturgies or sermons. The whole passage also bears a tone of tranquillity, in contrast to the sharp attack on a false philosophy in chapter 2. "Let the peace of Christ rule in your hearts" (3:15) seems a paramount injunction: The church will grow and prosper not by bickering or conflict, but by stable and resolute daily living in accord with the will of God as known in Christ.

Introductory Exhortation (3:1-4)

The form of this opening paragraph closely resembles that of 2:20-23. "If you have been raised with Christ" (3:1) parallels "If with Christ you died" (2:20), and the rejection of the Errorists' ethical norms (2:21-23) is balanced by a positive enunciation of those of the writer, which is adumbrated with the summary injunction, "Seek the things that are above" (3:1). The language of dying and rising with Christ is taken from baptismal ideas and imagery that have already been stressed in the letter to indicate the real but invisible foundation of Christian existence (see especially 1:13-14, 21-23; 2:11-13). The present short paragraph contains a series of parallel expressions and reduplications: seek . . . set your minds on (vv. 1, 2); things that "are above" (vv. 1, 2); you have been raised . . . you have died (vv. 1, 3); your life . . . our life (vv. 3, 4); seated at the right hand of God . . . in God (vv. 1, 3). These give extra emphasis to the paragraph's ideas; they also suggest that much of its phraseology may derive from liturgical traditions.

The "so" at the beginning of verse 1 does not refer to any single affirmation in the previous lines of the letter, but rather signifies that in general the definition of Christian responsibility to come is based on the theological affirmations of the first two chapters. Like 2:20, 3:1 begins with a conditional clause, "If you [plural] have. . . ." The author implies that the readers have a general understanding of baptism as dying and rising with Christ, and 2:12 already said explicitly that the rite involves burial and resurrection with Christ. The conditional clause in verse 1 is followed by a direct command to seek "the things that are above." This is repeated in verse 2 in positive and negative forms: Set your mind on things above, not on earthly things. In 3:1-4 three dualistic contrasts are underlined: the contrast between dying and rising (vv. 1 and 3), between things above and things on earth (vv. 1 and 2), and between present hiddenness and future revelation in glory (vv. 3 and 4). These binary contrasts, however, are not as simple as they might at first seem. The Error assailed in chapter 2 may have used similar language to encourage an otherworldly orientation, with the understanding that the "things that are above" pertain to unusual visionary experiences (2:18) and "the things below" to the present material world. The writer of Colossians, however, quickly makes it clear that he works with other definitions—for him the "things that are on earth" are immoral desires and actions (3:5-9) and the "things that are above" pertain to the hidden relationship with the exalted Christ and God that underlies Christian existence in the present world (3:10–4:6).

The "things that are above" exist at present and believers are firmly connected with them when they allow God as known in Christ to govern their lives on earth. There is a somewhat similar use of the term "above" (Gk. *ano*) in John 8:23; Gal 4:26; and Phil 3:14—but the phrase "things that are above" is unique in the New Testament. The general appeals to seek and think about "the higher things" are backed up by affirmations that believers have already shared in the death and resurrection of Christ, that they presently participate in Christ's (hidden) exaltation/ enthronement at God's right hand (compare Eph 2:6 and Rev 3:21), and that they can be confident of taking part in his future glorious revelation (his parousia). The image of Christ at the right hand of God derives ultimately from Ps 110:1 (cited, e.g., in Acts 2:33-36; Rom 8:34), but as usual the author of Colossians does not point out the link with Jewish Scripture and may use this language simply as a familiar expression of Christian belief (it may already have been part of the Christian liturgical tradition). It is suggestive that in 2:14-15 the writer did not cite Ps 110:1c to speak of the subjection of Christ's foes (in contrast to 1 Cor 15:25; Eph 1:22; Heb 10:13; and 1 Pet 3:22).

The spiritual attitude of "seeking" and "setting your minds" is, then, not substantially different from that indicated in Rom 12:1-2: Renewal of the mind is integrally bound up with an authentic lifestyle (cf. the emphasis on "hostile in mind" in 1:21 and on "knowledge" in 3:10). The transformed thinking is not so much attachment to abstract doctrines as it is a deliberate decision to "see things" from God's viewpoint, according to the purposes of God for human life revealed through Jesus Christ (1:9, 28; 2:2-3; cf. Matt 16:23; Phil 2:5). The frequent references to Jesus as Lord in the hortatory passage (3:13, 18, 20, 22-24; 4:1) are indications of how believers are to keep their thoughts oriented to the risen and exalted Christ. Their visible activities in the world are to be based on worship and prayer (see 3:16-17) and reasoning oriented to the "symbolic world" they have entered through baptism (Meeks 1993, 47).

The writer says that "your [plural] life" is presently concealed with Christ in God. (The angelic beings so prominent in 1:15-20 and 2:8-20 are left unmentioned in Col 3–4. The only superhuman powers that believers need to be concerned about are Christ and God.) The writer chooses an aorist tense for the verb for the event of dying with Christ (in baptism) but a perfect tense (implying lasting results) for the verb "hidden." The death is past, believers are already raised, exalted, and alive in Christ—yet their new existence is fundamentally "hidden." The meaning of this must be connected with the awareness that God and the Risen Christ are not visible to physical eyes. Faith here is assumed to be a matter of looking to "what cannot be seen" (2 Cor 4:18; cf. Heb 11:1, 27). The writer has already said that "all the treasures of wisdom and knowledge" are hid in Christ (2:3) and manifested only to believers (1:26). The message about God's will was formerly hidden from everyone, but now is manifest in the church. Still, there are hidden depths or treasures that perhaps even believers will not fully plumb until the eschaton. To outsiders they remain a closed book. Even to believers their true or essential "life" in the present time and world is understood here to be profoundly mysterious, in the realm of the unseen. The present hiddenness is contrasted in verse 4 with the glory to be revealed when Christ "who is our life" appears—an allusion to Christ's second coming (the only such direct reference in Colossians). The equating of Christ with life recalls John 1:4; 4:14; 5:26; 8:12; 11:25; 14:6; 20:31; Rom 5:10, 21; 2 Cor 4:10-12; Phil 1:21; 2 Tim 1:1; 1 John 1:1-2; 5:11-12, 20; Ignatius, *Eph.* 3:2, 7.2; *Smyrn.* 4:1; *Mag.* 1:2. This verse contains one of the letter's strongest references to future eschatology (though that will be stressed again in terms of judgment in 3:6, 24-25, 4:1). The meaning must be that through faith and baptism Christians are joined to Christ so deeply and fully that his life becomes their own—as he is hidden, so also are they; when he is revealed in the future, they will be revealed, and revealed in his company. The notion of the present hiddenness of those to be saved might appeal to persons familiar with pagan mystery cults or Gnosticism, but the moral conclusions of 3:5–4:6 drawn by the author point in different directions. As believers die to rise to new life, so they discover their "hidden life" by entering into life in the present physical world and giving themselves in love to their neighbors, in the first instance their neighbors within the community of faith. They find themselves by going out of themselves; and yet their true selves are not abandoned or lost, but only "hidden."

The clause "when Christ is revealed" by its very simplicity and calm conciseness suggests that the author and the Colossians are not breathlessly expecting the end or worried about its delay and the conceivable results of that delay (the tone of our passage is very different from that in 1 Thess 4:13-18). The earthquake that struck in the vicinity of Colossae around 60 CE (without apparently destroying Colossae itself) undoubtedly gave many people a bitter sense of the fragility of human existence. But the writer nowhere alludes to that tragedy and his eschatological teaching here lends no support to efforts to predict the return of Christ in relation to earthquakes or similar phenomena (in contrast to Mark 13 and Revelation). Verses 3-4 seem to echo and clarify the thought of 1:27, that the entire Christian message can be summed up as "Christ in [among] you, the hope of glory."

There is a variant reading for verse 4 that would make it speak of "our life" rather than "your [plural] life." There is such good manuscript support for both readings that either is possible, and both make good sense in the passage. The general emphasis on "you" (plural) favors "your" here; but the ease with which the letter in other passages shifts back and forth between first-person plural and second-person plural (1:12-14; 2:13-16)—and a concern to emphasize to the readers that Paul and all believers share in the situation of the Colossian Christians—favors "our life."

◊ ◊ ◊ ◊

The spiritual life of Christians with Christ through death and resurrection in baptism is not something visible; nevertheless, it is the decisive reality in their lives, determinative of all else. The author presumably could have written "with Christ and God" or "in Christ and God." Christ is not simply equated with God, yet believers have a life in God because of their relationship with Christ. Their future hope is conceptualized here, as often in the undisputed letters, as a life in the presence of Christ (Lona 1984, 181). Their present heavenly exaltation is based not on what they can do but on what Christ has already accomplished and made available to them through faith and baptism. It is not based on exotic spiritual experiences like those claimed by the Errorists, according to 2:18. Yet it is a genuine heavenly ascent shared by all church members, and it is "ontological" in the sense that it asserts where the true being of believers is to be found (cf. Wilson 1997, 130-31).

Related to its concern to affirm the total adequacy of what Christ has accomplished already, Colossians tends to emphasize "realized eschatology" (a concept of salvation as already available at the present time) rather than a view that salvation will be gained only in the future. It has been pointed out that the letter tends to replace temporal categories (now/then) with spatial ones (earth/heaven), as in 3:1-4 (Conzelmann 1979, 92-93). Yet there is an "eschatological reserve" in the language of concealment and revelation in 3:3-4. That which is now hidden shall one day be manifested—clearly on the day of Christ's parousia. The concept of believers being revealed in glory at the last time links this text with several other New Testament passages that speak of believers reigning with Christ or sharing his divine splendor in the future (cf. Matt 13:43; 19:28; John 17:24; Rom 8:29-30; Phil 3:21). The idea that they are presently leading a concealed life may imply for this author that at present they do not fully understand themselves (cf. 1 John 3:1-2) and are not well understood by others.

There is a clear implication of total security. One can understand how a medieval Christian mystic, very likely recalling this passage, wrote, "Rest on the hidden foundations of your soul" *(Theologica Germanica).* Although the physical death of believers does not seem to be a primary source of controversy in Colossae (in contrast to 1 Cor 15 and 1 Thess 4), our passage implies that physical death should hold no terrors: Believers have already undergone death with Christ, and they will certainly share his future glory in a life beyond the present one (cf. Rom 8:18-39). While the writer does not overtly cite Jewish precedents, the idea of being hidden by God and thereby given transcendent protection resonates with various Old Testament passages (e.g., 1 Kgs 17:3; Ps 91:1-2; Isa 51:16; Jer 36:26).

It is particularly important that within the structure of Colossians this bold affirmation of the heavenly existence of believers functions as the introduction to the letter's exhortations about conduct. Believers are, as it were, citizens of two worlds (cf. Phil 3:20), and their roles and responsibilities in the here and now rest on their invisible foundation. The writer of Colossians is no advocate of religious escapism or noninvolvement in the material world—in contrast to the "philosophy" assailed in chapter 2. On the other hand, neither does he suggest that believers have already arrived at perfection. Though Christ has already triumphed over all hostile powers (2:14-15) and already delivered believers from the power of darkness (1:13), believers must recognize that, in a sense, the darkness lingers within them. The author's eschatology is complex, and it guards against any enthusiastic assumption that church members are free from sin. In his essay "Of Experience," Michel de Montaigne remarks that people who want to rise above the human condition and live in this world as though they were angels often combine "supercelestial thoughts and subterranean conduct." The author of Colossians does what he can to prevent that from happening.

Putting Off the Old Being and Putting On the New (3:5-17)

This passage sets forth negative and positive moral standards that apply to all believers. The particular vices and virtues mentioned seem not to be related to particular problems at Colossae. On the other hand, the entire passage (like the rest of 3:1–4:6) emphasizes responsible living in the present world in a way drastically different from the approach of the Errorists.

The dominant image in the passage is that of putting off the Old Being and putting on the New, imagery based on baptism (though baptism is not explicitly mentioned here) and plainly connected with the thought of 2:11-15.

Table 3: The Structure of 3:5-17 (AT)

Negative Commands	Transformation to Recognize	Positive Commands
	(C) You have put off the Old Being with its practices ... and put on the New Being ... where there is neither Greek nor Jew ... but Christ is all and in all (vv. 9b-11)	
(B) Put away all these things: anger, wrath ... (vv. 8-9a)		(D) Put on, therefore, compassion, kindness ... (v. 12)
(A) Put to death, therefore, whatever in you is earthly: sexual immorality, uncleanness ... (v. 5)		(E) Bear with one another and forgive each other ... put on love ... let the peace of Christ ... (vv. 13-17)

First the author summarizes desires and deeds that are incompatible with life in Christ; these are to be "put to death" (3:5) or gotten rid of (3:8; cf. 2:11). He proceeds to set forth positively the things that life within the community of believers requires; these are attitudes and patterns of interaction to be "put on" (3:12, 14). In the center of this section—a brief set of indicative affirmations interrupting the series of imperatives—is a confession about existence in Christ (as in 3:1, 3-4): Believers have already (in baptism) put off the Old Being and put on the New (3:9b-11). The implication then is, as in 3:1-4, that they should live out the consequences of their already-established "new identity" in Christ. They should "be what they are." They should resist inclinations to revert to their pre-Christian ways of life (v. 7) and struggle to appropriate a new lifestyle just because they have "already" through faith and baptism put off their former nature and put on the "New Being."

Two lists of five nouns naming vices (3:5, 8) dominate the presentation of wrongful desires and actions, and these lists are supported by brief warranting statements (vv. 6-7) and explanations (vv. 5c, 9). One list of five nouns naming virtues is presented (v. 12) followed immediately by a second list of seven more positive actions expressed with verbal clauses (vv. 13-17) and supported by concise warrants (vv. 13b, 14b, 15b) and elaborations (vv. 16b, 17b). No obvious effort has been made to make vices and virtues correspond. While verses 5-15 concentrate on ethical responsibilities, verses 16-17 emphasize worship and "do[ing] everything" in relation to Christ and God the Father.

Some of the major theological ideas that support the imperatives are those of future divine judgment for wrongdoing (v. 6), God's choosing and calling of those in the body of the church (vv. 12, 15), the Lord's forgiveness (v. 13) and—above all—the new creation in Christ (vv. 10-11). The distinctively Christian elements in the passage appear especially in the warrants and "metaphorical framework" (Meeks 1993, 48-49).

Many details within the passage probably reflect the use of traditional materials, especially the virtue and vice lists (Fitzgerald 1992) and the christological confession in verse 11.

The use of virtue and vice lists as means of moral instruction was common among pagans and Jews before early Christians took up the practice, and Paul's undisputed letters already contain some notable instances (Virtue Lists: 2 Cor 6:6-7a; Gal 5:22-23; Phil 4:8; Vice Lists: Rom 1:29-31; 13:13; 1 Cor 5:10-11; 6:9-10; 2 Cor 12:20-21; Gal 5:19-21). Philo's writings offer some interesting parallels, both in vice and virtue lists (e.g., *Ebr.* 21, *Virt.* 180-82). Probably the idea of describing the Christian life as an extension of baptism was established at any early date. Yet there seems to be no model in any earlier non-Christian or Christian document for the structure of 3:5-17 as a whole, and we may detect a certain awkwardness of phrasing in some of its subsections, especially verses 9*b*-11. This suggests that the integration of the whole was part of the innovative contribution of the writer of Colossians.

Putting Off Old Vices (3:5-9*a*): The emphasis of this passage is on what the Christian life excludes—that is, those appetites and activities that characterize the realm of darkness from which believers have been delivered in Christ (1:13, 21) or, to use another image, "the body of the flesh," which has been stripped off in baptism (2:11).

Based on what has just been asserted in 3:1-4 (to which a "therefore" points back), verse 5 instructs the readers to kill "whatever in you is earthly" (the same Greek phrase has appeared in v. 2). These "members" are not parts of the physical body (in contrast to the use of the term in, e.g., Matt 5:29 30; Rom 6:13; 7:5; Jas 3:5-6; 4:1)—here the term refers to sinful desires and behavior, as the author proceeds at once to make clear. The command to "put to death" in verse 5 implies that the offending passions are still alive and dangerous in believers (cf. Rom 8:13). That such warnings were typical of Pauline parenesis is apparent from Rom 13:12-14—also using baptismal imagery of casting off and putting on (cf. the "vice lists" in 1 Cor 6:9-11 and Gal 5:19-21). The fivefold list of vices here and in verse 8, over against which a fivefold list of virtues is set in verse 12, suggests a traditional pattern of moral instruction that may ultimately stem from Iranian traditions linking cosmology and ethics (Schweizer 1982a, 182-87). In verse 5, sexual immorality is stressed first, then uncleanness in general, passion and evil desire; at the end of the list comes "greed," which the author says is equivalent to worship of false gods. That explanation suggests a Jewish background (within which worship of any deity but the God of Moses was the basic transgression). Similar links between covetousness and idolatry are made in *T. Judah* 19:1; Philo, *Spec. Leg.* 1.23; and Pol. *Phil.* 11:2. The five terms for vices may allude to behavior, but they also emphasize inner desires of individuals.

The first term in the vice list, sometimes translated as "fornication" (Gk. *porneia*) probably refers to sexual misconduct in general. Emphatic warnings against sexual misconduct are typical of ancient Jewish and Christian teaching (e.g., 1 Cor 5:10-11; 6:9-10; 2 Cor 12:21; Gal 5:19-21; Eph 5:3; 1 Thess 4:3; 1 Tim 1:9-10), but they are by no means unfamiliar in pagan moral exhortation. The vices identified by "impurity," "passion," and "evil desire" would easily suggest sexual associations, but there seems no strong reason to limit their sense here in that fashion. "Passion" must mean strong desire for wrongful objects, not strong desire in general. The emphasis of verse 5 on evil desire recalls the warning of the Sermon on the Mount (Matt 5:27-28), and the violent language (obviously meant metaphorically) of "put to death" recalls the language of mutilation in Matt 5:29-30. The author does not seek or expect Christians to eliminate all physical or sexual desires, but he assumes it is possible to control them.

The term "greed" seems quite general, and a reader familiar with the Decalogue of Moses would think of the final commandment. "Beware of covetousness" is a frequent admonition in the New Testament (Matt 6:24 par.; Mark 7:22; Luke 12:15; Rom 1:29; Eph 5:3). Yet the writer of Colossians never speaks of any lingering relevance for Christians of the Law of Moses (in contrast to Rom 13:8 and Gal 5:14). Why is covetousness equated with idolatry? Perhaps the sense is: Covetousness essentially means desire of what does not belong to you with an implication of willingness to exceed the bounds of God's order so as to acquire it—hence it means to worship something in place of God. Like the addressees of Rom 1:20-28, the anticipated readers of Col 3 are assumed to instantly reject anything equated with idol-worship.

The writer then adds two notes regarding these evil desires. First (v. 6) he asserts that God's wrath is coming because of these things (all the vices listed in v. 5); the reference is clearly to condemnation of evil at the future Last Judgment (to which v. 4 has already alluded; cf. Rom 1:18; 2:5-11; 1 Thess 1:10; 2:16). (The phrase "on the children of disobedience" is included in some good manuscripts for v. 6, but the phrase was almost certainly added for clarification by a later scribe who was influenced by Eph 5:6. Moreover, it suggests that believers should separate themselves sharply from non-Christians, an idea that is not sounded elsewhere in Colossians and that seems to conflict with 4:5-6; cf. 1 Cor 5:9-13.) In verse 7 the writer remarks that the readers once (i.e., before they were baptized) lived in accord with these vicious desires, an allusion to their former hostility to God and sinful behavior (as in 1:21). The exhortations, however, imply that their present life "with Christ in God" does not render them immune from temptation.

In verse 8 the writer instructs them to put away "all such things," and proceeds to offer a new vice list, one that emphasizes human wrath and deception. This group of five terms may be rendered "anger, wrath, evil, abusive speech, and shameful language." Again we are reminded of the Sermon on the Mount (Matt 5:21-26, 33-36). As in verse 5, the list emphasizes inner feelings (anger, wrath, malice) alongside outward words (slander, foul talk, lying). The mention of an apparently additional vice in "Do not lie to one another" in verse 9a, like the phrase "which is idolatry" in verse 5c, gives the instruction a special orientation to the church. Presumably the writer does not mean to condone lying to non-Christians (cf. 4:5-6); rather, as in verses 12-17, the Christian community is assumed to be the primary environment of Christian living.

◊   ◊   ◊   ◊

You Have Already Put On Christ (3:9b-11): The two aorist participles in verses 9-10 ("stripped off" and "clothed yourselves") are best understood as asserting what has already in fact happened: through faith and baptism all believers have already stripped off "the Old Being" (and the vices associated with it, specified in 3:5, 8-9a) and put on "the New Being" (with the appropriate way of life to be detailed in vv. 12-17). (The term rendered here as "Being" [Gk. *anthropos*] could also be translated "human being" or "nature" or "self" [the rendering in the NRSV]. "Being" perhaps suggests the personal and corporate implications of the term better than the alternatives.)

The language in 3:10 resembles Paul's words about the new creation in Christ (2 Cor 5:17; cf. Gal 6:15). The language of new creation is surely derived from Christian reinterpretation of Gen 1:26-27 (cf. *Barn.* 6:11-12), but the writer of Colossians as usual does not make the link with the Jewish Bible explicit. Similar "Old Being" language is used in Rom 6:6 and 1 Cor 5:7 and is later taken up in Eph 4:22. The New Being is described as going through a process of renewal in knowledge according to the image of God, an image that has already been identified with Christ (1:15). It is evident that the "New Being" refers to both every individual convert and to the church regarded as a corporate eschatological entity "nearly identical with Christ himself" (Dahl 1976, 134). Statements about "being renewed" and "its creator" are appropriate for individual believers and the church, but they do not fit Christ well (Jervell 1960, 243-44). A generation or two after Colossians was written, however, Ignatius of Antioch applied the term "New Being" directly to Christ (*Eph.* 20.1).

"According to the image of its [the New Being's] creator" (3:10) apparently means that Christ is the image of God, but God the Father is the one who creates (re-creates) the believer as "the New Being." The thought here is like that of Rom 13:14; Gal 3:27; and Eph 4:24. As Christ is the image of God, so all Christians bear his image (cf. the future-oriented statements in Rom 8:29; 1 Cor 15:44-49). As believers bear Christ's image, they will be transformed not only in their conduct but also in their knowledge (Gk. *epignōsis*—as in 1:9, 10) of God's will for their lives.

Diogenes the Cynic philosopher said that "good men are images [Gk. *eikones*] of the gods" (Diogenes Laertius, *Vit. Phil.* 6:1). Philo sometimes interprets the rational soul of human beings as being made in the image of the Logos, which in turn was created in the image of God; and it is the presence of a copy of the divine Logos in every human being's mind that gives her or him the capacity to overcome such dangerous passions as those listed in 3:5 and 8 (see, e.g., *Leg. All.* 1.31-42; *Abr.* 243-44). Their creation-based relationship to the Logos of God, which is the image of God, is also the basis of their ability to have genuine *knowledge* of God (cf. Plato, *Theaetetus* 176A-177A). Philo can also speak of the Jewish people as carrying the images (Gk. *eikones*) of the commandments of Moses in their souls (*Gaium* 210). For the author of Colossians, Christians carry in their souls the image of Christ, which gives them true knowledge of what is pleasing to God (cf. 1:9-10). No mention is made of believers being guided by any law.

The phrase "in that renewal" in verse 11 must refer to the New Being (and to every local community of believers). Here old distinctions between human groups no longer matter: distinctions between Greeks, Jews, barbarians, Scythians, slaves and free persons. The terms used for human groups suggest that all ethnic, religious, and legal distinctions cease to matter in relation to Christ. Very similar expressions occur in two passages in the undisputed letters: 1 Cor 12:12-13 and Gal 3:27-28. The combination of similarities and differences has suggested to many scholars that we have here a traditional church formulation, probably part of the baptismal liturgy (baptism involves "putting on Christ" in Gal 3:27) celebrating Christian conversion as a new beginning for humanity (Meeks 1993, 46). Christ brings about a kind of reconciliation of opposites, in this case of opposed human groups.

The term "Greek" in the Colossian passage could mean "Gentile" (non-Jew)—as in Rom 1:16. It may, however, allude to the special pride Greeks felt for their cultural tradition as representing the acme of human greatness, comparable to the pride Jews felt in their nationhood. The phrase "circumcised and uncircumcised" seems redundant, though it might allude to the divine ordinance of Gen 17 supporting Jewish particularism (cf. Gal 6:15). The naming of Greek before Jew here, in contrast to the order in 1 Cor 12:13 and Gal 3:28 (and Paul's regular pattern of naming Jews first—Rom 1:16; 2:9-10; 3:9, 29-30; 9:24; 10:12; 1 Cor 1:24) suggests that Colossians represents a stage in church development in which Gentile Christians predominate (Wolter 1993, 182).

The formula in 3:11 has an element lacking in 1 Cor 12:13 and Gal 3:28: explicit reference to the overcoming of cultural and ethnic or racial divisions (whereas the Jew-Gentile distinction was first of all a religious one). "Barbarians" suggests inarticulate speech and lack of culture and Greeks sometimes applied the term to non-Greeks in general (cf. Plato, *Statesman* 262E; Philo, *Vita Mos.* 2.12 [though Philo implies that Jews are a third group, neither Greek nor Barbarian]). "Scythians" may be mentioned as an example of uncivilized living (Josephus says they are close to wild animals—*C. Apion* 2.269; cf. Philo's *Gaium* 10). A case can be made, however, that in the area around Colossae the term "Scythian" would imply "civilized person" in contrast to an uncultured "barbarian" (Martin 1995; cf. Malherbe 1977, 6-7; 48-51). The terms "slave" and "free" must refer to the legal status of individuals.

How is this assertion "Christ is all and in all" to be understood? Stoics could speak of the world as encircled and ruled by God (e.g., Cicero, *Nat. Deor.* 1.39). An invocation of the Egyptian goddess Isis runs "You Isis, a goddess, you are all things!" Although Ben Sira assumes the traditional Jewish understanding of God as distinct from his creation, he can sum up his praise of God by declaring "he is the all" (43:27) (Barth and Blanke 1994, 417). In 3:11 the phrase "and in all" implies Christ's union with believers (1:27; cf. Gal 2:20); but in the light of 1:15-20 the author probably intends it to bear a larger significance. The sense of this striking phrase seems to be that Christ is Lord over all in the universe and in the church and also lives as "the New Being" in every believer (cf. Eph 4:10). (An almost identical phrase in 1 Cor 15:28 speaks of the end-time total sovereignty of God; the emphasis in 3:11 is on the present-time dominion of Christ; cf. 1:13.) The concept of Christ presently ruling over believers' lives will be stressed more in the rest of the parenetic section than elsewhere in the letter (nine of the letter's fourteen uses of the term Lord [Gk. *kyrios*] to designate Christ occur in 3:13–4:1).

The affirmation in verse 11 that Christ's presence "in all" obliterates human distinctions hints that the worldwide preaching of the gospel is a preaching of universal equality and brotherhood and sisterhood. As God through Christ has brought about a universal reconciliation (1:20), and just as Christ holds the entire universe together (1:17), so everyone is somehow related to the image of Christ, which is the image of God. Christ is the face of God in every human heart. However, that face is concealed from all who lack faith. (Thus 3:11 hints at a new division within humanity, one between those inside the church and those outside; yet it does not draw that line directly, and 1:20 may—in accord with our earlier interpretation of that verse—imply that the unity and reconciliation of all persons exist quite apart from the faith appropriations of human beings.) Still, it can also be said that Christians in this passage are summoned to think of the Christian community as an "alternative world" (Lindemann 1983, 58), pointing the way toward humanity's ultimate future.

The thought is not that every human is Christ or that Christ is an archetype or universal symbol of self-realization or self-integration, but rather that, through faith and dying and rising with him, people in the church have taken on the nature or image of Christ, which is the image of God. This image makes them all spiritual equals, though 3:11 hints that they remain aware of their differences. In 4:11 Paul will indicate that he is very conscious of his Jewishness and that of three of his companions, and in 3:22–4:1 he will make it clear that differences between slaves and masters continue not only in consciousness but in outward conduct and obligations.

Verse 11 suggests a divine promise of the universal reconciliation of peoples, which echoes not only 1:20 but also broad tendencies in contemporary, especially Stoic, pagan philosophy (see, e.g., Cicero, *On Ends* 3.62-68) and some branches of Judaism (see Philo, *Joseph* 28-31; *Vita Mos.* 2.17-20; *Virt.* 119-20). (See further Taylor 1992; Bassler 1982, 105-19, who notes ways in which ideas of universalism could be combined with old and new distinctions between human groups.)

Putting On New Virtues (3:12-17): This passage summarizes the positive attitudes and actions that Christian faith requires of all church members, regarded as individuals, balancing the desires and conduct that verses 5-9 indicate are to be overcome. The verb "to clothe," already used with an indicative sense in verse 10, is now used as an imperative to indicate the new way of life believers must embrace (similar uses of the verb are found in Rom 13:12, 14; Eph 6:11, 14; 1 Thess 5:8; cf. Matt 22:11). A conjunction meaning "therefore" (Gk. *oun*) in verse 12 matches similar ones in 3:1, 5; although it may have a general reference to 3:1-11, it probably refers primarily to the assertions in verses 10-11 (the imperative "clothe yourself" of verse 12 builds on the assertion "you have clothed yourselves" in v. 10).

Church members are described as "elect [chosen] by God," "holy," and "beloved" (cf. Rom 8:33; 2 Tim 2:10; Titus 1:1; 1 Pet 2:9). The term "elect" shows that the status of believers stems from a divine decision (as does the expression about "called in the one body [of the church]" in 3:15. The origin of the Christian life is God's calling, and this idea points toward the emphasis on thankfulness at the end of the paragraph (vv. 16-17). The term "elect" is used widely in the Old Testament regarding Israel or the portion of Israel destined for salvation, and the use of "elect" here without the definite article leaves open the possibility that there are persons presently outside the Christian community who are also God's "elect." In the New Testament the term is used of those destined to be saved (with emphasis on future salvation) in Matt 22:14; Mark 13:20, 22 (parallels in Matt 24:22, 24); Luke 18:7; Rom 8:33; Rev 17:14. The use of the term in the plural to describe all Christians seems particularly characteristic of the Deutero-Pauline writings (2 Tim 2:10; Titus 1:1; 1 Pet 1:1; 2:9).

The term "holy" has already been applied to church members as such four times (1:2, 4, 11, 26), a usage familiar in many other Pauline passages (Rom 1:7; 1 Cor 1:2; 16:1; 2 Cor 1:1; 13:12; Eph 1:15; 3:18; 5:3; Phil 1:1; Phlm 5). The use here particularly recalls the work of Christ to present believers "holy and blameless" before God (presumably at the last judgment) in 1:22. Hence their holiness is primarily a gift, though it also implies a demand that believers "walk worthily of the Lord" (see 1:9-10, 12).

The use of "beloved" here resembles the same use of the verb in the passive in Rom 9:25; 1 Thess 1:4; 2 Thess 2:13 (cf. the use of "loved" in Eph 2:4; 5:2, 25—portraying the Christian community as the object of the love of God or Christ). In 3:12 God is the one who loves, just as God is the one who elects. Colossians does not elsewhere explicitly speak of the love of God or Christ for humanity (though 1:13 speaks of God's love for the Son). The letter uses "beloved" in several passages where it seems to refer only to believers' love for individual church members (1:7; 4:7, 9, 14), though the thought of God's love is probably in the background. Persons familiar with the Jewish Scriptures would readily think of their association of election and divine love (as in Deut 4:37; 7:6-13; 10:15; Isa 43:4; 54:8, 10; 55:3; 63:7-9; Jer 31:3; Hos 3:1; 11:1, 4).

The five virtues that Christians are to "put on" in verse 12 all seem to combine inner attitudes and outward behavior. They also pertain to good conduct in relation to other persons (within the Christian community), just as the vice list in verses 8-9a stressed anger and abusive speech directed at others (whereas the vice list in v. 5 could be understood to apply to individuals in isolation). The virtues commended in verse 12 fit well with the more explicitly Christian injunctions to follow in verses 13-17, although several of the same virtues are also emphasized in Stoic lists (see, e.g., Epictetus, *Discourses* 2.22.36, which urges tolerance, gentleness, kindness, and forgiveness). The terms "humility" and "meekness" denote virtues exercised in relation to other Christians (as in Rom 12:3, 16; 1 Cor 13:4-5; Gal 5:23; 6:1; Phil 2:1, 5). Humility, especially in relation to other human beings, is not typically honored in pagan writings; but it is emphasized in some late-Jewish materials (e.g., 1QS 2.24; 4.3-4; *m. Abot* 4:4). Perhaps there is an allusion to the false humility associated with angelic worship in 2:18; there may also be an allusion here to sayings in the gospel tradition (e.g., Matt 18:4; Mark 10:42-44). Together with verses 11 and 14, this verse outlines a general ideology of humility and unity within the church, but—as 3:18–4:1 will make evident—not one of social equality in the modern sense (Osiek and Balch 1997, 102).

Verse 13 expands the instruction with special attention to reacting to the misdeeds of other believers. Christians are to be patient with one another's faults and forgive them out of remembrance that their own salvation can be summed up as God's forgiveness through Christ (1:14; 2:13; a close parallel is found in Eph 4:32). The sense seems clearly: "As the Lord has forgiven you, so you [must also forgive others]." Imitation of Christ's forgiveness (at the core of the message of salvation—1:12-13, 20, 22-23; 2:13) is not optional or supererogatory. This seems close to the concept that God's forgiveness of us is conditioned on our forgiveness of others as stressed in the Gospels (Matt 6:12, 14-15; 18:21-35; Mark 11:25; Luke 6:37; 11:4; 17:3-4). One may reasonably surmise that in the early Christian communities there existed frequent need to hear a message about the necessity of forgiving other believers, and the undisputed Pauline letters attest this (see, e.g., Rom 12:17-21; 2 Cor 2:5-11; Gal 6:1-2; Phlm 17-18).

Despite the strong emphasis on forgiveness, the writer proceeds to speak of love as a kind of additional duty—and one that is supreme, "above all" (v. 14). This demand for love is explained or warranted by the assertion that "it binds everything together in perfect harmony" (or is a "bond [Gk. *sundesmos*] of perfection"). This probably is meant to recall the statement in 1:17 that the entire creation is held together through Christ, as well as that in 2:19 that church unity and growth depend on holding fast to Christ. The concept of love here seems definitely christological: The same love of God manifest in Christ (1:13; 3:12), which is a kind of cosmic force for cohesion, is now echoed in the chief obligation of Christians. The church will be held together by the extension of Christ's love. The active practice of forgiveness and love toward other Christians is essential for church unity and the attaining of Christian maturity (1:28). There may be an implied polemic as well: In contrast to the elitist achievements emphasized by the "deceitful philosophy," mutual love is the key to maturity (Lindemann 1983, 61). Love is also held up as the supreme Christian virtue as in Mark 12:28-34 par.; John 13:34; Rom 13:10; 1 Cor 13; Gal 5:14; 1 Pet 4:8; 1 Clem. 49 (which may allude to Col 3:14 in speaking of the "bond [Gk. desmos] of the love of God" in relation to church unity). Ancient Pythagoreans described love between friends (Gk. philia) as "the bond [Gk. sundesmos] of all the virtues" (Lohse 1971, 148). Plato stated that the idea of the good can serve as the bond (Gk. sundesmos) of unity among different and opposing parts of virtue in a political community (Statesman 310A).

With verses 15-17 we arrive at "theological virtues" or modes of thinking and acting that involve more than interhuman relationships. Allowing the peace of Christ to rule and letting the word of Christ dwell inwardly (vv. 15-16) seem built on the conviction that Christ came to reconcile all things to God. He reconciles Christians to God (1:21-22), but this must be extended into interrelationships among believers so that they may fulfill their calling to be "one body." This is the only reference to the church as "one body" in Colossians (cf. the somewhat different uses of that phrase in Rom 12:4 and Eph 2:16). Here the point is that the Christian community in Colossae (and, by implication, all Christian communities) must and can be united through the reconciling peace that Christ brought to the world and that Christians must permit to "rule" their minds, words, and deeds. (The term for letting peace "rule" [Gk. brabeuein] in this verse surely deliberately echoes the term for the Errorists' divisive judgments [Gk. katabrabeuein] in 2:18. These are the only uses of these terms in the NT.) Also the readers are required to be thankful. Thanksgiving (directed apparently to Christ or God) is a major theme in this letter, stressed here and in 1:3, 12; 2:7; 3:16-17 and 4:2. Only here in the New Testament is the adjective "thankful" (Gk. eucharitos) employed, and the very simplicity of the formulation in verse 15 suggests that it has a comprehensive sense: The whole of the Christian life should be a thankful response to God's work of peacemaking in Christ.

Verses 16-17 conclude the section with language that sets all the exhortations in the context of worship. The word of Christ is to permeate believers' lives, and all their actions are to be performed in relation to God and Christ. The phrase "word of Christ" occurs nowhere else in the New Testament; it is, however, well attested and is probably the correct reading, although some manuscripts have "word of God" or "word of the Lord" instead. The emphasis on "the word of Christ" probably is meant to emphasize that the life and worship of believers is grounded in the confession concerning God's work of salvation in Jesus. The phrase in verse 16 probably means primarily the message about Christ (the gospel about his loving work of reconciliation brought about through his death—cf. 1:20-22; 2 Cor 5:18-21; Eph 2:14-16). The phrase could also be the message and words of Jesus (grammatically a genitive of author or origin) as known in the Gospel tradition, with which (as we have seen) much of the exhortation in 3:1-17 agrees (cf. Eph 4:20-21). Perhaps even the reading of a Pauline letter (as in 4:16) could provide "the word of Christ." "Let the word of Christ dwell in you" (3:16) implies obedience to the "word," expressed especially in teaching and admonishment (cf. 1:28).

The word of Christ is also linked here with "all wisdom" (cf. 2:2-3). This anticipates the injunction in 4:5 to act toward outsiders with wisdom, which on a minimalist interpretation implies prudential caution. In 3:16 "wisdom" must refer to the entire life of the Christian community, not least as it gathers to sing in praise of God. Verse 16 may also allude to the main components of an early church worship service: proclamation and teaching of the message of Christ, exhortation and admonition (as in 3:5-15), singing of hymns, prayers of thanksgiving. But the reference need not be restricted to formal worship services.

It is not clear if the author intends to distinguish three different kinds of religious songs with the terms "psalms," "hymns," and "spiritual songs." That they are to be sung "in your hearts" and directed to God's hearing implies that this "singing" need not always involve outward sound and may go on apart from communal worship gatherings. Yet music is seen as a valid and valuable means of praising God, as it was in the Jewish tradition (see Acts 16:25; 1 Cor 14:15, 26; Eph 5:19). Singing also suggests the "hymn" in 1:15-20 and the wisdom about creation and redemption that underlies Christian behavior (cf. Epictetus, *Discourses* 1.16.16-21; 3.26.29-30). The earlier affirmations about the union of believers with Christ (3:1, 3-4, 10-11) are now qualified or interpreted in terms of submitting to the revelation of Christ and allowing it to penetrate deeply into the lives, songs, and hearts of church members.

Verse 17 also has a tone of concluding generality: All Christian words and deeds are to bear witness to Christ and God. Everything is to be done in the name of the Lord Jesus, and thanksgiving is to be continually offered through him to God the Father. A generation or two after Colossians was written (around 110 CE), a Roman governor of Bithynia in Asia Minor, Pliny the Younger, reported that the Christians he interrogated gathered to sing hymns "to Christ as to a God" (*Letters* 10.96 § 7). If their hymns were like those described in 3:16-17, we may suppose that Pliny missed a subtle but vital point: Christians recognized a distinction between God the Father and Jesus, but they also understood that they were offering worship to God through Jesus as Lord (cf. Phil 2:11).

◊ ◊ ◊ ◊

This passage about putting off an old life and putting on a new one illustrates how early Christian exhortation overlapped in content and style significantly with contemporary pagan and Jewish instruction. The putting off of the "Old Being" did not mean that all pre-Christian moral ideas were fallacious.

There is a notable blend of perfectionism and pragmatism in the passage. No room for merely partial realization of the virtues is indicated in verses 12-17. Yet the norms are not defined as laws that any community could easily enforce, and the naming of the virtues leaves much room for Christian moral reflection and individual decisions about implementation. The vices are discussed in verses 5-9*a* as patterns of desire and action to be utterly eschewed as incompatible with the Christian life. Yet the imagery of "putting to death" and "putting off" implies that temptations persist for members of the Christian community, none of whom is expected to be perfect. The "New Being" is an eschatological ideal, but it is also one in process of present realization in the community of those who think of themselves as having already risen to new life in Christ.

Appropriately, in the middle of the passage are the evocative statements about putting off not patterns of conduct but "the Old Being" and putting on not patterns of conduct but "the New Being." Although the details in the concept of the new creation are not neatly specified, the overall sense seems clear: Christ is the standard or "image" of the life to which all Christians are called. The Law of Moses is not recognized as a norm, however much it may have historically influenced the definition of vices listed in 3:5-8. Christ is at one point cited as an example (v. 13), but the primary idea of "all and in all" (v. 11) seems to be that Christ lives within believers and does so as Lord of all aspects of their lives (v. 17). It is possible that there are some deliberate allusions to traditions about Jesus' life and teachings in the unusual phrase "the word of Christ" (v. 16), and it would not be difficult to draw a connection between teachings and narratives eventually written down in the New Testament Gospels and the individual vices and virtues emphasized in this passage. Colossians does not clearly intend readers to do that. But Christ has the dominant place in 3:5-17, and the community of Christ is defined here in terms of individuals recreated in knowledge in accord with Christ's image. That image is partly defined by the patterns of life believers are to take on according to verses 12-17, but it is also defined by the understanding of Christ's power and function as divine image in universal creation and reconciliation (1:15-20).

The claim that "Christ is all and in all" and that national and religious divisions no longer exist for Christians must also be seen as a fulfillment in the realm of salvation of the claim that Christ has reconciled to himself all things, whether on earth or in heaven, making peace through his death (1:20). Exactly what the ending of these divisions means for the daily lives of believers is not explained, though it is a fair assumption that Paul means to imply that all the interpersonal virtues mentioned in verses 12-17 are to be practiced in the Christian community without regard to old prejudices based on religious, national, or legal boundaries. The inclusivist vision of verse 11 may also be understood to explain the missionary efforts of Paul and other evangelists assumed throughout the letter, efforts that the Colossians are obviously expected to approve and support. Yet that vision stands in obvious tension with the divisions between household groups mentioned in 3:18–4:1, and it is unlikely that Paul and the Colossians failed to notice this.

Duties Defined by Position in a Household (3:18–4:1)

This passage has great structural clarity and an appearance of being self-contained, suggesting literary independence from what has gone before. Also, if it were deleted, 4:2 would follow 3:17 smoothly. Since Martin Luther it has been customary to refer to this passage as the "Table of Household Duties," meaning a section defining ethical responsibilities according to position within a household (including the position of slaves). Similar or related passages are found in Eph 5:22-6:9; Titus 2:2-10; 3:1-2; 1 Pet 2:13-3:7; 1 Clem. 21:6-8; Ign. Pol. 4:1-6:2; and Pol. Phil. 4:2-6:1. The "Household Table" in Colossians is the first known to us, and the literary pattern may have been invented by the author of Colossians, building on traditional materials and cultural preconceptions about the value of a patriarchal order.

There is no clear indication that the passage was shaped with special needs in Colossae in mind: Like the injunctions in 3:5-17, those of the Household Table would apply in almost any ancient Christian community. The exhortations are general and leave much room for interpretation; they also take no account of particular circumstances or potential conflicts with other requirements (like 3:17) that might set limits on the submission or obedience demanded. Yet it is possible that the lengthy instructions to slaves reflect a particular situation in the Colossian church, one in which enthusiasm about unity and equality in Christ made some think Christianity was incompatible with slavery (Crouch 1972, 149-51).

Nevertheless, 3:18–4:1 has clear connections with earlier parts of the letter. Coming after verses 5-17, which present moral defects all believers must "take off" and moral qualities all believers must "put on," 3:18–4:1 clearly is meant to define moral obligations varying according to relationships within a household. At the same time, it seems likely that the author intends this passage to provide some examples of how in the everyday world believers should go about living in relation to their faith in God and Christ (3:17). Since the house-church was probably the basic cell in the Christian movement (Meeks 1983, 75-77), it is not surprising that household relationships would seem a proper sphere and source of examples for explaining Christian duties. The passage certainly does not cover all possible household relationships and responsibilities—for example, those of unmarried brothers or sisters of a household head. Likewise, the stress on reciprocal duties suggests that Paul is addressing persons living in Christian households. No consideration is given, for example, to Christian wives with non-Christian husbands, or Christian slaves having to deal with non-Christian masters—though such situations must have been fairly common in the first century (cf. 1 Pet 2:18-25; 3:1). Contemporary non-Christian teachings often cover obligations to siblings, friends, homeland, and government. It may be significant that Colossians has nothing to say about duties toward the state (in contrast to Rom 13:1-7 and 1 Pet 2:13-17).

The passage divides straightforwardly into three sections, dealing respectively with the relationships of wives and husbands (3:18-19), children and parents (3:20-21) and servants and masters (3:22–4:1). Each group is addressed directly in the second-person plural. In each group, the inferiors are spoken to first and then the superiors. The passage affirms reciprocity: Inferiors and superiors have different but corresponding duties, because all are bound to Christ as Lord. Yet the commandments to inferiors are not made conditional on the good behavior of superiors, or vice versa. The following chart puts things somewhat out of order, but brings out salient similarities and differences in the instructions and the warrants used to support them:

Table 4: Inferiors and Superiors in 3:18–4:1

Persons Addressed	Basic Instruction	Religious Warrants or Qualifications
Inferiors: 3:18 Wives	Be subject to your husbands	as is fitting in the Lord
Inferiors: 3:20 Children	Obey your parents in all things	for this is pleasing in the Lord
Inferiors: 3:22-25 Slaves	Obey your human masters in all things—not giving only outward service as pleasers of human beings, but with sincere hearts—whatever you do, do it from your soul	Fearing the Lord—knowing that from the Lord you will receive the compensation of the inheritance—you are serving the Lord Christ—for he who does wrong will be paid back for the wrong, and there is no partiality
Superiors: 3:19 Husbands	Love your wives, and do not be embittered toward them	
Superiors: 3:21 Fathers	Do not provoke your children, lest they become discouraged	
Superiors: 4:1 Masters	Treat your slaves justly and fairly	Because you know that you also have a Lord in heaven

Wives are told to "be subject" to their husbands, children and slaves are told to obey in "everything." The lengthiest instructions by far are given to slaves. All of the commands to inferiors are backed up by religious warrants, most of which refer to Christ as Lord. Only those given to slaves directly mention divine judgment, rewards, and punishments. Slaves, like wives and children, are addressed as responsible individuals with feelings, ideas, and rights.

As all the "inferiors" are told to accept subordination, all the "superiors" are told to exercise their authority with restraint and kindness (husbands and fathers) or justice (slave owners). None of the superiors are told to exercise ruling authority; this is presupposed. The passage also presupposes that persons of power within the community of faith need to be warned against abusing their "inferiors." Perhaps the length of the exhortation addressed to slaves is an indication that some Christian slaves find their service onerous to the point of being intolerable.

The injunctions with their direct addresses to the various groups appear to assume there are church members in all six categories. Probably the groups overlap: Women might simultaneously be wives, parents, and slave masters. Men might be husbands, sons, and slave owners. The same individual might be a superior in one relationship and an inferior in another.

No close formal parallels to this passage have been found in ancient Jewish or pagan writings. In terms of content, however, there are numerous passages in the works of pagan writers that speak of the duties of superiors and inferiors in households (see Aristotle *Politics* 1253b-1259b: "The primary and smallest parts of the household are master and slave, husband and wife, father and children . . ."). A branch of philosophy was developed to treat the topic of "household management." Seneca (*Letter* 94.1) speaks of the part of philosophy offering "specific prescriptions for every role in life . . . for advice which is dispensed to the husband regarding his demeanor toward his wife, to the father regarding his rearing of his children, to the master regarding how he should rule his slaves" (note that Seneca offers no corresponding advice for the wives, children, or slaves).

Because the right ordering of the household was widely thought to be the foundation of order in society, the emperor Augustus gave his official support to this patriarchal value system. One of his advisors, the Stoic philosopher Arius Didymus, justified it in terms of mental capacity: "The man has the rule of this house by nature. For the deliberative faculty in a woman is inferior, in children it does not yet exist, and it is completely foreign to slaves" (quoted from Balch 1981, 42). Josephus says the subordination of women is based on natural inferiority ordained by God: "The woman, says the law, is in all things inferior to the man. Let her accordingly be submissive, not for her humiliation, but that she may be directed, for the authority has been given by God to the man" (C. *Apion* 2.199).

It seems probable that a hellenistic-Jewish pattern of teaching lies in the background of the Colossian Household Table (Crouch 1972, 119). An especially interesting passage written by Philo interprets the Decalogue commandment about honoring parents to contain

> a suggestion of many necessary laws formulated to deal with the relations of old to young, rulers to subjects, benefactors to benefited, slaves to masters. For parents belong to the superior class of the pairs already mentioned, that which comprises seniors, rulers, benefactors and masters, while children occupy the lower position with juniors, subjects, receivers of benefits and slaves. And there are many other instructions given, to the young on courtesy to the old, to the old on taking care of the young, to subjects on obeying their rulers, to rulers on promoting the welfare of their subjects, to recipients of benefits on responding to them with gratitude, to those who have given of their own initiative on not seeking to get repayment as though it were a debt, to servants on rendering an affectionate loyalty to their masters, to masters on showing the gentleness and kindness by which inequality is equalized. (*Decal.* 165-67; cf. *Spec. Leg.* 2:226-27)

Philo mentions instructions given to both inferiors and superiors, which is what we find in 3:18–4:1. He does not, however, mention in this passage the reciprocal obligations of wives and husbands. In another passage Philo speaks of superiors offering benefits through religious instruction: "The husband seems competent to transmit knowledge of the laws to his wife, the father to his children, the master to his slaves" (*Hypothetica* 7:14). The Greek word for "partiality" in 3:25 is rare and only attested in Christian writings, but it appears to derive from a Hebrew idiom found in Deut 10:17. This is another bit of evidence that something like the Household Table in Colossians already existed in Jewish tradition. However, the writer of Eph 5:22–6:9 obviously felt that explicit references to the Old Testament needed to be added.

In content, if not in form, the author of Colossians is presenting in this passage moral teaching that must have reminded many readers of contemporary pagan and Jewish values. Yet 3:18–4:1 offers some relatively unusual features in keeping with Christian presuppositions: (1) much of the teaching is directly addressed to subordinate groups (wives, children, and slaves); (2) there are emphatic warnings to husbands, fathers, and masters not to misuse their authority; and (3) there are explicit warranting references to "the Lord" (Christ) in verses 18, 20, 22-24; 4:1, sometimes in connection with the Last Judgment. Despite all its references to human "superiors," this brief passage also contains exactly half (seven) of all the references to Christ as Lord in the entire letter.

Wives and Husbands (3:18-19). Women are told to "be subject" to their husbands. Plainly this is instruction only for married women. Further, married women are not told to be in subjection to males in general, but only and specifically to their husbands. As we shall see, later on (4:15) the writer sends greetings to a woman church leader in Laodicea ("Nympha"), with no suggestion that she is in any kind of subordinate position. The command "be subject" seems to have a less sweeping meaning than the "obey" given to children and slaves. Also wives are not told to submit "in everything," as are the children and slaves.

The phrase "as is fitting in the Lord" seems to be a Christian modification of the Stoic ethical idea of duty as what is "fitting." The term for fittingness is used in a similar way in Eph 5:4; Phlm 8; *1 Clem.* 62:1. The idea of discerning and doing what is "fitting" in a moral sense is expressed with other terms in Matt 3:15; Acts 22:22; Rom 1:28; 1 Cor 11:13; Eph 5:3; 1 Tim 2:10. The addition of "in the Lord" can hardly be a trivial qualification for Paul or the Colossians. "In the Lord" suggests not only motive but also limitation: The wife's ultimate "lord" is not her husband. Colossians does not, however, explicitly raise the problems faced by a Christian wife living under the same roof with a pagan husband (in contrast to 1 Cor 7:13-16 and 1 Pet 3:1-6) or other cases in which a wife might, on grounds of conscience, feel compelled to oppose her spouse's wishes. About a century later Tertullian gives a vivid description of the difficulties faced by a Christian woman married to a pagan, contending that "she certainly cannot fulfill the teachings of the Lord, since she has at her side a servant of the devil, who will act as an agent of his lord to obstruct the duties and pursuits of believers" (*To His Wife* § 4). Plutarch expresses a typical (especially male) pagan view in saying that wives should follow the religion of their husbands (Plutarch, *Praec. Conj.* 140D).

The Jewish tradition offered varied views of the status of women and wives. Thus Tob 8:4-7 suggests a relatively egalitarian position, speaking of Sarah, Tobias's wife, as his "helper and support." Philo says that "wives must be in servitude to their husbands," though he adds that this should not be based on violent ill-treatment (*Hypothetica* 7:3).

Husbands are commanded to "love your wives and do not be embittered against them" (AT). It is striking that the command to the husbands is more focused on inner feelings, whereas that to wives could be interpreted as emphasizing outward submission. The term for love (Gk. *agapan*) is the verb corresponding to the noun used in 3:14. Without developing the elaborate comparison with Christ and the church present in Eph 5:25-33, the writer of Colossians calls on husbands to practice in their most intimate personal relationships the kind of unselfish caring required of Christians in general (O'Brien 1982, 223; Schrage 1990, 254). The expression about bitterness could mean either that husbands should not allow themselves to become angry or bitter toward their spouses or that they should not treat them with harshness (so the NRSV). Certainly a husband embittered against his wife would not love her in a Christian sense and would not act toward her with the kindness and forbearance that 3:12-13 demands. The superior power or authority given husbands by civil law and custom (and assumed or legitimated by the author of Colossians in 3:18) could itself tempt husbands to feel or show anger toward their spouses: A wife's vulnerability might arouse brutality. Our passage's unqualified approval of marriage and its assumption of the inequality of the partners reveal attitudes rather different from those expressed in 1 Cor 7.

Some rabbinic and pagan writers warned against misogyny and displays of anger toward wives, presumably because they were not uncommon. Plutarch criticizes men and husbands who "rage bitterly against women" (*On the Control of Anger* 457A), but that writer also asserts that husbands must control their wives—"not as the owner has control of a piece of property, but, as the soul controls the body, by entering into her feelings and being knit to her through goodwill" (*Praec. Conj.* 142E). Philo assumes that husbands should care for their wives unselfishly (*Post. Cain* 181). Pseudo-Phocylides (a hellenistic-Jewish writer of perhaps the first century CE) advises husbands, "Love your own wife, for what is sweeter and better than whenever a wife is kindly disposed toward her husband and a husband toward his wife till old age, without strife divisively interfering?" (*Sentences* 195-97; cf. Wilson 1994, 142).

Children and Parents (3:20-21): Children are told to obey their parents (not just their fathers) "in everything," this being explained and justified as their "acceptable duty in the Lord" (similar expressions are used to describe the entire Christian life in 1:10; Rom 12:1, 2; 14:18; 2 Cor 5:9; Eph 5:10; Phil 4:18). The implication is that children's devotion to Christ is manifest as they obey their mothers and fathers. The writer seems to call for unlimited obedience, though perhaps the reference to pleasing the Lord is understood to set some limitations (cf. O'Brien 1982, 225). Philo implies limits when he writes that children should obey their parents "in everything that is just and profitable" (*Spec. Leg.* 2:234-36).

In verse 21 fathers are addressed: "Do not provoke your children, or they may lose heart." (The term translated here "fathers" may refer to both parents, as it does in Heb 11:23.) The reference to discouragement probably implies that the children are young, though conceivably adult children are also in view (Roman law gave fathers great power over children of any age). Pagan writers also said that parents should discipline their children in honorable ways (e.g., Plato, *Laws* 793-94), and Pseudo-Plutarch writes that "children ought to be led to honorable practices by means of encouragement and reasoning, and most certainly not by blows or ill-treatment" (*Education of Children* 8F). In Jewish tradition we also find admonitions not to be harsh with children. Pseudo-Phocylides advises, "Do not apply your hand violently to tender children" and "Do not be harsh with your children, but be gentle" (*Sentences* 150 and 207).

Slaves and Masters (3:22–4:1): Now attention is turned on the reciprocal responsibilities of slaves and their masters. Contemporary non-Christian writings, both pagan and Jewish, do not ordinarily directly address, or refer to, slaves as morally responsible persons (Crouch 1972, 116-17). The writer of Colossians instructs slaves to offer obedience "in everything." The reference to "your earthly masters" distinguishes their authority from the ultimate lordship of Christ. Yet any sharp disjunction is immediately overcome by the demand that slaves provide service to their human masters "fearing the Lord" and "as done for the Lord and not for your masters" (vv. 22-23). This is taken even further in the direct statement of verse 24c: "You serve the Lord Christ." They are to obey earthly masters in such a way that they thereby serve Christ. More than that, they are to work "wholeheartedly" (literally "from your soul") whatever their tasks, keeping their minds focused on the thought that they are thereby serving their heavenly Lord. (Slaves were acquired and maintained so that they might do work, and they showed obedience primarily as workers; children and wives are called to submission and obedience more generally.)

At this point Colossians suggests a strong appreciation of the dignity of work done with single-mindedness to please God, not to please human beings (especially human masters). The reader may be meant to recall Paul's emphasis on his own hard labor for God and the churches (1:29).

Colossians can use slavery as a metaphor for the service all Christians (or at least church leaders) are called to render (1:7; 4:7, 12), though it does not portray Christ himself as a "slave" (in contrast to Phil 2:7). The injunctions to work hard at serving the Lord and not men might seem particularly well suited to slaves, since Greco-Roman culture tended to regard it as improper for free men to take orders from anyone except their fathers or military commanders and also to regard regular work, especially manual work, as "not fitting" for citizens (Cicero, *Off.* 1.150).

The basic thought, then, of 3:22-25 is that Christ himself requires that Christian slaves serve their human owners. The final sentence in verse 24 is probably an imperative rather than an indicative: "Serve Christ!" This command, however, along with the injunction not to work as pleasers of human beings (v. 22) at least suggests that sometimes reverence for Christ should lead a Christian slave to refuse the command of her or his human owner. The idea of rendering service to Christ is coupled with an eschatological promise that Christ will give "the inheritance as your reward" (an after-death heavenly compensation making up for the fact that Roman law did not permit slaves to inherit anything; cf. 1:5). Finally a warning is given: Those who act unjustly will receive an appropriate punishment from Christ, at whose judgment seat there is no partiality (v. 25). Since slave masters are not directly addressed until 4:1, the warning would most naturally seem to refer to misconduct on the part of slaves. But probably there is an implicit word of comfort to slaves as well: The wrongdoing of anyone, masters included, will receive fitting punishment at the hands of the heavenly judge. (Ephesians 6:9 rephrases the statement in Col 3:25 so that it becomes entirely a warning to masters.) There is more emphasis on eschatological judgment in 3:24–4:1 than anywhere else in Colossians, and this suggests an understanding that the slave-master relationship was an area of life in the real world where injustice was commonplace.

In a single sentence (4:1) slave masters are told to consider ("know") the fact that they are accountable to a heavenly lord. (Probably the brevity of teaching for masters reflects the fact that there were far more slaves than masters in early Christian congregations.) Bearing Christ in mind, masters must treat their slaves with "justice and equality" (AT; the word for "equality" may also be translated as "fairness"). The notion that justice applies to slaves marks a departure from the tradition of Aristotle (*N.E.* 1134b). Perhaps alluding to Pythagorean teachings, Philo remarks that "the mother of justice is equality" (*Spec. Leg.* 4.231; cf. *Plant.* 122). As for slaves, Philo says that no one is naturally a slave (*Spec. Leg.* 2.69) and speaks admiringly of the Essenes and Therapeutae, Jewish groups that repudiated slavery on principle (*Vita Cont.* 70; *Every Good Man is Free* 79). Yet Philo himself considers slaves essential to ordinary urban life (*Spec. Leg.* 2.123). Pseudo-Phocylides also assumes Jewish ownership of slaves, and simply counsels masters to treat them humanely (*Sentences* 223-27).

◊ ◊ ◊ ◊

The entire set of household instructions has a worldly character in the sense of defining Christian responsibilities in daily life. It is probably correct to see in these seemingly unadventurous guidelines a quiet but resolute countering of the escapist tendency and ascetic counsels of the Errorists attacked in Col 2. Yet there is also a positive message that does not hinge on the Error: Believers are counseled to affirm life in the present world and accept structures of social order generally taken for granted by nonbelievers. As Christ rules the universe, so believers' obligations toward Christ are now explained in relation to everyday domestic experiences.

Although the instructions in 3:18–4:1 are all addressed to Christians, they would remind believers of hierarchies and values in the non-Christian world. One can well imagine that many ancient non-Christians, apprised of the teaching in the Household Table, would feel bound to approve the exhortations to both inferiors and superiors, perhaps seeing in Christianity simply a new basis or sanction for maintaining traditional values and social structures of subordination. Various scholarly theories have been developed to explain the rise of moral instructions like this Household Table within the early church on the basis of unstated functions or purposes (e.g., a desire to defend Christians against the charge of upsetting the social order, and perhaps thereby attract converts—cf. Thurston 1995, 60-61). To the extent that the equality in Christ implied in 3:11 was confessed and honored in Christian communities, questions about eliminating different roles and levels of obedience were bound to arise inside and outside those communities. It seems likely (though unprovable) that part of the motivation for this Household Table was to inform believers and potential critics from the outside that Christianity did not mean social upheaval. (For an unusual interpretation arguing for Christian equality in relation to this passage, see Standhartinger 1999, 247-76.)

Perhaps part of the "hiddenness" of the Christian life as the writer conceives it lies in the outward similarity of Christian subordinationist teaching to that which pagans of the day might assume. The life in Christ is "hidden" in the sense that Christian allegiance to a new Lord will only become fully visible at the Parousia (3:4). Of course there are dangers when people of faith strive in principle to be inconspicuous.

Yet all of these injunctions to submit and obey are understood to be "in the Lord." Part of the sense of "Christ is all and in all" of 3:11 is surely that obedience to Christ redefines by implication the limits and possibilities of obedience to human authorities. It is by no means inconsequential that the general injunctions to put on a new life in Christ (3:5-17) precede the hierarchical instructions in 3:18–4:1, which might seem to simply rubber-stamp pre-Christian norms. Clearly the author of the Household Table was no social revolutionary, although one can make a case that he desacralized worldly authority structures in such a way as to indirectly prepare for radical change (Pokorný 1991, 184). While the general emphasis of the passage is on "inferiors" giving complete submission to "superiors," the emphasis on Christ as ultimate Lord implicitly reminds the readers that worldly authorities wield only a relative power and that believers may sometimes have to disobey earthly masters in order to remain faithful to Christ.

The passage stresses further that Christian husbands, parents, and slave owners need to be warned against abusing their power. These human "superiors" are not equated with Christ, and 3:18–4:1 does not say that household power structures are part of an eternal order legitimated by God and Christ in creation and redemption. Slave masters are not identified as God's representatives (in contrast to *Did.* 4:11). Furthermore, believers are reminded that one day all earthly superior-inferior relationships will pass away and everyone will have to give an account in a courtroom of Christ (4:1; cf. 2 Cor 5:10).

The author of Colossians does not here forbid slaves to seek their freedom or deny that they can have significant leadership roles in the church (see below on 4:9). He does not repudiate what Gal 3:28 says about women or deny that women can be church leaders (see below on 4:15). He does not argue that subordination is justified because of any natural or divinely decreed mental or moral inferiority of women to men, children to parents, or slaves to the unenslaved.

Still, the writer does urge submission and obedience, and these teachings provided some basis for subsequent centuries of Christian acceptance of slavery and oppression of women by men, especially within marriage. Colossians combines a sweeping message of liberation from all superhuman rulers (e.g., in 2:14-15) with a socially conservative acceptance of existing authority structures (D'Angelo 1994, 322; cf. Fiorenza 1984, 252-54).

In this passage the writer of Colossians appears to assume that these hierarchical structures are part of the everyday (first-century) world that Christians must in a measure accept if they intend to participate in household relationships. At the same time he offers some guidance on how Christians can strive to maintain their religious integrity whatever their positions. In all their experiences of control and subordination in this world, believers should try to discern and respond to the will of their heavenly Lord.

Prayer and Witness to Outsiders (4:2-6)

These verses conclude the parenetic section of the letter. By a few references to Paul's present situation, they also provide a transition to the personal greetings and instructions with which the letter ends (4:7-18). The author no longer singles out special groups within the church, as in the Household Table (3:18–4:1) but now addresses all church members, as in 3:5-17. Whereas the instructions of 3:5–4:1 focused on life inside the Christian community, 4:2-6 turns the readers' attention to communication with non-Christians. Paul asks the Colossians to support with prayer his desire to preach the gospel despite his current imprisonment. Then he gives instruction about how they should themselves communicate with outsiders.

Fairly similar closing general admonitions are found in 1 Gal 5:26–6:6; Phil 4:8-9; and Thess 5:12-22. The primary exhortations are those in verses 2 and 5 (each combine an imperative with a participle). Warrants are not directly mentioned in this section, apart from the "as I should" in verse 4*b*. Paul's request for prayer for his personal situation interrupts a series of compressed imperative clauses in 4:2, 5-6, as it does the flow of general imperatives that began in 3:1.

◊ ◊ ◊ ◊

The final set of general instructions is initiated by a summons to pray with persistence and thanksgiving. The concept of prayer in Colossians implies that everything finally depends on God's power, and that Christians need to be reminded to believe this. Thanksgiving has been a frequent theme in this letter (1:3, 12; 2:7; 3:15-17), and the emphasis on it in 4:2 reminds the recipients of the letter that genuine prayer must express gratitude for gifts already received and not simply consist in petitions for the future. In 1:9 Paul wrote that "we" (he and Timothy) pray for the Colossians ceaselessly (cf. 1:3), and the same will be said about Epaphras in 4:12. The command to hold fast or continue in prayer appears in almost identical wording in Rom 12:12. Calls for constant prayer also appear near the conclusions of letters in Eph 6:18; Phil 4:6; and 1 Thess 5:17.

The thought of "keeping alert" in prayer is not linked here with any direct word about the Parousia, but the term in early Christian usage could easily suggest the thought of final judgment and limited opportunities (Mark 13:34-37; 1 Thess 5:6, 10; 1 Pet 5:8). Likewise, the expression "making the most of the time" in 4:5 would probably have overtones for many early Christians of the end of the world and the need to use limited time well in relation to God's redemptive purposes (cf. John 9:4). Ephesians 5:16 seems to express the same essential thought with the words "[make] the most of the time, because the days are evil." (Colossians, however, characteristically does not suggest that the present age is dominated by evil.)

Paul tactfully requests prayers for himself before reminding the Colossians that they also have responsibilities toward outsiders. In verses 3-4 Paul requests special prayers for "us" (the first-person plural presumably alludes to Timothy, but it may also refer to all those individuals to be mentioned as being with Paul in vv. 7-14). Paul hopes that God may "open . . . a door" for him to preach the gospel as he ought. (Similar prayers for Paul and his work appear at the end of other letters: Rom 15:30-32; Eph 6:19-20; 1 Thess 5:25; 2 Thess 3:1-2.) Paul seeks prayers not for his personal comfort but for his missionary activity. Paul seeks prayers not only that he may have missionary opportunities but also that he may reveal "the mystery of Christ" as he should. The phrases "a door for the word" and "the mystery of Christ" obviously refer to the church's basic missionary message (cf. 1:26; 3:16). The image of an "open door" as a symbol of an opportunity to preach appears also in Acts 14:27; 1 Cor 16:9; and 2 Cor 2:12. Given the brevity of the expression, we cannot know if Paul hopes for release from prison or some opportunity to bear witness in his present situation (cf. Phil 1:12-14). The Colossians are asked only for their prayers, but their prayers for Paul (along with their remembrance of such Pauline coworkers as Epaphras and Onesimus) will keep the issue of missionary outreach in their consciousness.

Why does Paul switch from "us" and "we" to "I" in verses 3-4? Probably he wants to emphasize his imprisonment (not all his coworkers are prisoners), but perhaps he also does not care to suggest that those coworkers might also fail to speak clearly! Verse 4 is the only suggestion of uncertainty that Paul expresses in the entire letter, and the uncertainty is not about anything in interpretation of the gospel but only about his own adequacy in proclaiming it. Perhaps verse 4 is more an expression of humility than of actual uncertainty. Such humility obviously sets a good example for the apostle's readers (cf. 3:12).

The reference to what Paul is "bound" to here alludes to his sense of God's commissioning of him as an apostle: He is constrained to speak the divine word (cf. 1 Cor 9:16-17). The Greek terms in verses 3-4 for "in prison" (dedemai) and "should" (dei) are based on the same root, indicating constraint or necessity. Paul is presently in chains (4:18) because of human rejection of his gospel, but the necessity and "bonds" that he is chiefly mindful of are the result of God's commission. The Colossians are probably expected to ponder the irony of a person "bound" by both God and humans, though for opposed reasons.

The brief mention of Paul's obligation to reveal the gospel to outsiders leads into brief instructions about how the Colossians should behave toward "outsiders" (v. 5—the same Greek expression designates non-Christians in 1 Cor 5:12-13 and 1 Thess 4:12). Despite the suggestion of hostility on the part of outsiders in Paul's reference to imprisonment (v. 3), the tone of verses 5-6 is irenic and nondefensive. Christians are understood to live in a realm of "light" sharply separated from the "darkness" of the non-Christian world (1:13); and those outside the light realm face condemnation (3:6). Yet the boundary line can always be crossed. There is no indifference toward, or hatred of, those outside. Church members are enjoined to communicate effectively and appropriately with non-Christians, though the form of their witness is expected to be different from that of "professional" missionaries like Paul. Apparently they are to prepare in advance how to respond to questions from outsiders (cf. 1 Pet 3:15, which, however, suggests answering accusations). The phrasing of verse 6 resembles that of a rabbinic maxim, "Be alert to study the Law, and know how to answer a free-thinker" (*m. Abot* 2:18). Clearly the "answering" is related to the message of the gospel.

The language of verses 5-6 is concise and allusive. The Colossians are told to make good use of their time and to speak with "wisdom" (Gk. *sophia*), "grace" (Gk. *charis*), and "salt." These three terms could be meant in quite general ways, so that the thought would be that believers need to be prepared to speak to outsiders with something like ordinary prudence, graciousness, and wit. Various commentators have suggested that the meaning is that Christian speech should be both wise and pleasant, neither insipid nor sentimental. Recognizing salt as a valuable flavoring and preservative for food, Plutarch speaks of conversations that are gracious and pleasantly saltlike (*Concerning Talkativeness* 514F; cf. *Table-Talk* 684E-685F; Malherbe 1977, 94-95).

On the other hand, believers might give these three terms more religious weight, thinking of the wisdom of God in Christ (1:9, 26; 2:3; 3:16) that understands creation and reconciliation in universal terms (1:20; 3:10). Likewise "grace" might prompt church insiders to recall that no one has earned salvation (1:6, 12). The reference to salty speech in verse 6 is unique in early Christian literature (cf. Eph 4:29 and Ign. *Mag.* 10:2), but it may allude to sayings of Jesus preserved in Matt 5:13 and Mark 9:49-50. Since 4:5-6 is surrounded by words about Paul (vv. 3-4) and the ongoing efforts of many persons involved in his missionary enterprise (vv. 7-17), probably the simple directives in verses 5-6 do have theological depth. To speak suitably to outsiders, Christians must be strong in their faith convictions and sensitive to the questions that existence poses for all human beings (cf. Hübner 1997, 116).

Paul does not ask for prayers that his suffering may be eased, only that he may receive an opportunity to go forward with his missionary work. Likewise he bids the Colossians think about their own opportunities and methods of bearing witness to Christ. Paul's phrasing has a low-key tone, but it reflects the spirit of a tireless and versatile missionary. Both he and the Colossians are in bondage, but their essential bondage is to the will of God. In telling the Colossians how they ought to answer everyone, Paul uses the Greek term *(dei)* for "ought" in verse 6 that he used in verse 4 to speak of his own duty ("should").

◊ ◊ ◊ ◊

Colossians does not say that every believer should be an evangelist like Paul, but this passage does imply that every believer should act and speak in a way that makes the faith attractive to outsiders. By beginning this paragraph with instructions about prayer, the apostle may imply that speaking with God should precede and guide conversations with other people.

Colossians 4:2-6 and 4:7-18 imply a general openness to the non-Christian world as well as a sense of vocational distinctions. Paul and missionaries like him (such as his coworkers) seem to bear primary responsibility for evangelizing nonbelievers. The church of Colossae is obviously expected to encourage their efforts, although no specific support is mentioned apart from prayer. The sheer length of the instructions about the internal life of the Christian community (3:5–4:2), in contrast to the brief imperatives about communicating with outsiders in 4:5-6, implies that the primary duties of ordinary believers have to do with the development of their faith and love for one another. Still, internal and external growth are not unconnected. The impression made on insiders and outsiders over time by the church—a community at its best distinguished by strong convictions and unifying ideals maintained along with forbearance and openness to all persons—must have been decisive for the survival and expansion of Christianity (cf. Gager 1975, 129-32, 140; Meeks 1983, 166-70).

LETTER CLOSING (4:7-18)

A recent study of the final sections of the undisputed Pauline letters emphasizes that they give clues to the general purposes of those letters. The letter closings contain such elements as these: concluding exhortations, greetings from Paul and persons with him as he writes, an autograph (a passage written by the apostle himself, after most of the letter has been dictated to a secretary), a peace wish, and a grace benediction (Weima 1994). The major elements in the closing section of Colossians are: a commendation of the men who carry the letter and who can convey personal information about Paul's situation (vv. 7-9), greetings to the church at Colossae from individuals in Paul's company (vv. 10-14: three Jewish and three Gentile Christians), a request that the Colossians convey Paul's greetings to the believers in Laodicea and to Nympha and the church in her house (v. 15), instructions about reading and exchanging letters and encouraging Archippus (vv. 16-17), an autograph including a reminder about Paul's imprisonment, and a grace benediction (v. 18).

There are two references to "God" (vv. 11, 12), two to "the Lord" (vv. 7 and 17), and one to "Christ Jesus" (v. 12). There is no attempt to summarize ideas about salvation and ethics developed in the previous chapters (in contrast to Gal 6:11-17), though the description of Epaphras's prayer (v. 12c) mentions issues of maturity and certainty that were important in chapters 1-2. Paul's authority as a reliable interpreter of the gospel is implied throughout the closing greetings and instructions. Given that the Colossians do not know Paul personally, the listing of persons with the apostle who send their greetings to Colossae, as well as the mention of two individuals in the church's vicinity (Nympha and Archippus), "serves the purpose of establishing

155

closer ties with the community" (Lohse 1971, 172). A number of these persons are also known in Colossae. These persons who send greetings are Paul's coworkers; it is likely that most or all of them are members of a missionary team headed by the apostle. Their greetings also suggest that they support what Paul has written. They are witnesses and guarantors of the letter.

Considering what was said in 3:11, it is striking that the letter closing names a slave free to serve the church (4:9), Jews and Gentiles working side by side in a common cause (4:10-14), and a woman church leader in the Lycus Valley who rates a special Pauline greeting (4:15). (Of course, unlike Gal 3:28, Col 3:11 fails to mention the overcoming of the male-female dichotomy. But that overcoming was part of the baptismal tradition that the author probably knew and did not repudiate.)

This closing section of the letter is not very similar in format to the ending of any of the other Pauline letters; only Romans and 1 Corinthians mention as many individuals. Similarities in coworkers who are named in Colossians and Philemon have persuaded some scholars that the two letters were written by Paul about the same time; others (e.g., Pokorný 1991, 189) infer that a Pauline disciple wrote Colossians and copied these names from Philemon. Like Col 4, Phlm 23-24 lists greetings from Epaphras, Mark, Aristarchus, Demas, and Luke (Archippus is mentioned in Phlm 2 and Onesimus in Phlm 10). On the other hand, Philemon does not mention Tychicus, Jesus Justus, or Nympha; and Colossians does not mention Philemon or Apphia.

Apart from the final chapters of Romans and 1 Corinthians, this is the longest passage in any of the Pauline letters dealing with final greetings and instructions. Eleven different individuals are named, all of them presented as associated with Paul, many of them (at least Onesimus, Epaphras, Nympha, Archippus, Aristarchus) known also to the Colossians. In contrast to Rom 16, most of the persons named in Colossians are with Paul as he writes; only two individuals are named as being in the vicinity of the addressees (Nympha and Archippus). Many are given short descriptions that praise them as responsible Christian leaders, but the effect of the passage as a whole (surely intentional) is to emphasize Paul's personal ties with the Colossians and so enhance his authority in writing this letter.

◊ ◊ ◊ ◊

The Letter Carriers and Their Unwritten News (4:7-9)

Paul's own situation of imprisonment is given special emphasis in 4:7-9 and 18, just as it was in 1:24 and 4:3. In 4:7-9 he three times mentions that Tychicus and Onesimus, who carry the letter to Colossae, can and will inform the church about how the apostle and those with him (including Timothy and the others named in 4:7-14) are getting along: "all the news about me" (v. 7), "that you may know how we are" (v. 8), "everything here" (v. 9). This repetition strongly suggests that Paul regards this personal news as important and he says it should "encourage your hearts" (v. 8). Almost his final words (v. 18) are "Remember my chains." Why does he not write about his situation in prison and the specific reason(s) for his arrest, or say anything about his prospects for release (in contrast to Phlm 22)? Perhaps going into details about the brutality of his treatment in prison (locked in with chains) would pose risks for Paul and the Christian friends who are with him, perhaps even risks for those who read or listen to his letter. Paul has emphasized that his suffering is real and important for the Colossians to keep in mind. Verses 7-9 show that he expects them to ask for a detailed oral report.

It is worth noting that many other things are left unsaid in 4:7-18. Some notable items are: the background of the injunction to receive Mark, the particular concerns Epaphras has as he struggles for the Colossians, why Nympha and those in her house are singled out for greetings, the rationale for exchanging letters with Laodicea, the assignment or ministry given to Archippus. The writer implies that the intended readers will already know the answers to these questions, or that they will query the individuals who bear the letter. The letter's allusions to important things that are not explained support the inference that Colossians is a genuine letter addressed to a real community: it is not simply an imitation of a Pauline letter.

Tychicus is called "a beloved brother, a faithful minister, and fellow servant in the Lord" (v. 7); Onesimus is only styled "the faithful and beloved brother, who is one of you" (v. 9). This language suggests that Tychicus has leadership qualities and experience not to be found (or not yet realized) in Onesimus. Yet both men can be trusted to give reliable and full news about Paul and his situation (v. 9). Tychicus is mentioned as serving as Paul's emissary in three other Deutero-Pauline passages (Eph 6:21; 2 Tim 4:12; Titus 3:12). Acts 20:4 identifies him as a native of Asia who traveled with Paul on his last missionary journey.

Onesimus is mentioned in verse 9 and in one other New Testament passage, Phlm 10 (though the entire letter to Philemon deals with his situation). From this passage and Col 4:9 scholars have usually deduced that Philemon (or Archippus) is (or was) the legal owner of Onesimus, a slave who sought help from Paul and whom Paul converted while in prison. Since Paul calls Onesimus "one of you" while writing the Colossians, the inference is that Onesimus is originally from Colossae and that Philemon resides in that city, along with Archippus (mentioned in Phlm 2 as Paul's "fellow soldier" and given special encouragement in 4:17). Assuming all this, we may wonder why no special greetings or encouragement are sent by Paul to Philemon and Apphia (perhaps his wife) and the church meeting in their home. One possibility is that the letter Paul sent to Laodicea (the "letter from Laodicea," mentioned in 4:16) is actually our letter to Philemon. That would imply that Philemon and Apphia live in that city rather than Colossae. If Philemon and Colossians were written about the same time by the historical Paul, the instructions and request concerning Onesimus in Philemon have to be seen in relation to the emphasis on Onesimus as Paul's agent in Colossians: Perhaps between the writing of Philemon and Colossians Paul received word from Philemon (or Archippus, if he was the owner of Onesimus) that Onesimus would be set free from slavery or at least allowed to serve Paul for a time in his missionary work. Around 110 CE Bishop Ignatius of Antioch writes to the Christian community at Ephesus, mentioning with high praise their bishop named Onesimus (Ignatius, *Eph.* 1:3;

2:1; 6:2). He may not be the same person mentioned in the Pauline letters, but that is surely a real historical possibility, especially since Ignatius's letter seems to be influenced by Paul's letter to Philemon (see Knox 1955).

Greetings from Paul's Coworkers (4:10-14)

When Paul moves on to name individuals with him who send greetings, he begins with three Jewish Christians (vv. 10-12) and emphasizes that "they have been a comfort to me." The word for comfort (Gk. *paregoria*) does not occur elsewhere in the New Testament; it came to have a quasi-medical meaning (Plutarch, *On Listening to Lectures* 43D; Philo *Quod Deus* 65; *Somn.* 1.12). Paul seems to explain his feeling of comfort by saying "they are the only ones of the circumcision among my co-workers for the kingdom of God." This could imply that Paul feels a special emotional bond with other Jewish Christians, though this would hardly be something to stress as he addressed a mainly Gentile church. More likely the implication is that Paul recognizes a continuity between the Christian message and the heritage of Abraham and Sarah, even though he has not in this letter explained that continuity or quoted from the Jewish Bible (cf. Barth and Blanke 1994, 482). The phrase "the only ones of the circumcision" implies, on the other hand, that some or many Jewish Christians do not support Paul. Barnabas and Mark had earlier separated from Paul, perhaps over theological as well as personal differences (Acts 15:37-39; Gal 2:11-14); now Paul is glad to claim them as partners (v. 10). The word for "co-worker" (Gk. *sunergos*) occurs only in 4:11 in Colossians, but the term is often used in the undisputed letters for Christian leaders commended by Paul (Rom 16:3, 9, 21; 2 Cor 8:23; Phil 2:25; 4:3; 1 Thess 3:2; Phlm 1, 24). The phrase "the kingdom of God" (used occasionally in the undisputed letters: Rom 14:17; 1 Cor 4:20; 6:9-10; 15:50; Gal 5:21) probably does not imply a distinction between that and the kingdom of the Son (1:13)—in contrast to 1 Cor 15:24-28, where the Son's kingdom is temporary (cf. Eph 5:5: "the kingdom of Christ and of God"). Paul may choose to speak here of "the kingdom of God" to imply a connection with the Jewish tradition in general; perhaps he also intends readers to catch an allusion to Jesus' teaching about the kingdom.

The emphasis on Aristarchus at the beginning of the group of persons sending greetings to Colossae (v. 10) suggests that he has special importance, at least among Paul's Jewish-Christian companions. He needs no introduction, apart from the note that he is a fellow prisoner with Paul. The brevity with which he is introduced suggests he is well known, whereas Mark and Jesus-Justus have to be further identified. Acts apparently refers to the same individual when it speaks of an Aristarchus who was a native of Thessalonica, who traveled with Paul, was threatened by an angry crowd in Ephesus, and accompanied Paul when he journeyed to Rome (Acts 19:29; 20:4; 27:2; cf. Phlm 23).

Mark is identified as a cousin of Barnabas, whose name is assumed to be well known. By implication Paul now seems to be on good terms with both, though the Colossians are evidently expected to understand that there was previously some grounds for not welcoming Mark. Since Mark is now with Paul and sends greetings, Paul is clearly reconciled to him. "Welcome him." The words imply that Paul has the right to give direct orders to the church at Colossae, and that if Mark visits Colossae he will do so as one of Paul's "co-workers" (cf. Phlm 24). The instruction to welcome him has previously been communicated to the Colossians, though we are not told how. The Pauline disciple who wrote 2 Tim 4:11 speaks of Mark very favorably, so later church tradition did not think in terms of any lasting estrangement between the two (even though tradition also said that Mark wrote the oldest Gospel on the basis of his association with Peter, not Paul: Irenaeus, *Adv. Haer.* 3.1; Eusebius *CH* 3.39).

Verse 11 provides the only information we have on the Jewish Christian identified as "Jesus who is called Justus." "Justus" is Latin for "the righteous one" and it was a fairly common honorary name among ancient Jews. It is given to Joseph Barsabbas in Acts 1:23, Titius in Acts 18:7, and James the brother of Jesus in Eusebius, *Church History* 2.23.4-18. Jews of Paul's day would ordinarily think the term implied "righteous in accord with the Law of Moses," but Paul does not directly raise that issue with the Colossians.

Epaphras, described earlier as "our beloved fellow servant" and "faithful minister of Christ on our behalf" (1:7) is now given the longest description of any of Paul's fellow workers as "a servant of Christ Jesus" who constantly prays for the Colossians' spiritual maturation and who has worked diligently for them as well as for believers in Hierapolis and Laodicea (vv. 12-13). Since the Letter to the Colossians as a whole may be understood as a call for growth into maturity (1:28-29), one can regard it as part of the answer to Epaphras's prayers. Paul and he presumably agree on what the Colossian believers need to hear. Why, then, does Paul not name Epaphras (as well as, or instead of, Timothy) as helping to write this letter? Why does he not send Epaphras back to Colossae along with Tychicus and Onesimus? Above all, why does Paul apparently need to commend or defend Epaphras's labors in prayer and work for the Christians in Colossae and the other two cities? Possibly Epaphras cannot travel because he is also a prisoner (cf. Phlm 23). It may be that Epaphras was not able to help the apostle formulate this letter even though he could provide a trustworthy report of the condition of the Colossian church. Perhaps he needs Paul's commendation because some in Colossae have found the ministry of Epaphras inadequate particularly in regard to the crisis generated by the Errorists.

In verse 14 Paul briefly passes along the greetings of two other Gentiles with him: "Luke, the beloved physician, and Demas greet you." Luke is also mentioned positively as one of the apostle's fellow workers in Phlm 24 and 2 Tim 4:11; Col 4:14 is the only text that identifies him as a physician. Like Mark, Luke was later credited with authoring a New Testament Gospel (Irenaeus, *Adv. Haer.* 3.1.1), but Paul says nothing about literary aspirations. Demas is the only individual sending greetings who is given no descriptive tag or praise; probably he needs no introduction to the Colossians, and no censure is implied. Later

Christian tradition, however, represented him as having treacherously abandoned Paul (2 Tim 4:10; see also the apocryphal *Acts of Paul* 3.1, 4, 12-14, 16).

Paul's Personal Greetings and Final Instructions (4:15-18)

In verses 15-18 Paul turns from reporting the greetings of others to say a few final things for himself. First he tells the Colossians to convey his greeting to the "brothers and sisters" in Laodicea. This is the only passage in the New Testament in which a community of Christians in one city is told to send greetings to a church in another city (the closest parallel is Rom 16:5, where the Romans are instructed to greet the church in the house of Prisca and Aquila—but that church is presumably also in Rome).

The Colossian Christians are further told to greet in Paul's name "Nympha and the church in her house." (The Greek term for "Nympha" could refer to either a woman or a man, and some manuscripts read "his house" rather than "her house"; other manuscripts read "their house." The best manuscript evidence favors "her house" and understanding "Nympha" as feminine, however. Probably the variant readings "his house" and "their house" arose because later Christian generations found it hard to imagine that a woman could be a church leader.) Nympha is not mentioned elsewhere in the New Testament. We can only presume that she was well known to the Colossians as the leader, or at least patron/host, of a particular congregation either in Laodicea or Hierapolis (Gnilka 1980, 244, 248; Gielen 1986). The very brevity of the greeting suggests that Paul and the Colossians take it for granted that women can be church leaders. Since this is the only individual to whom Paul sends greetings, it is reasonable to suppose that he knows Nympha personally and respects her leadership. Perhaps there is a hint that she will support the teaching of this letter (Lindemann 1983, 77; but cf. Collins 1995, 174-79). Apparently most Christian meetings took place in private homes in the first and second centuries, and a large house might accommodate as many as a hundred persons.

References to house-churches appear in three other Pauline passages (Rom 16:5; 1 Cor 16:19; Phlm 2).

Public reading of Paul's letters is reflected in 1 Thess 5:27 and Phlm 2. Paul does not explicitly say the churches of Colossae and Laodicea are to have the letters read aloud in public worship, but that seems a fair inference from 4:16. Obviously this implies that both letters are important for both communities. Probably we can infer that the Errorists in Colossae had won a hearing in Laodicea.

The greatest mystery in verse 16 is, of course, the "letter from Laodicea." Is this a letter Paul has sent *to* Laodicea, one that will be "from" Laodicea when it arrives in Colossae? Or is it a letter that the Laodiceans themselves have written? And why are no arrangements mentioned for either letter to be read also in Hierapolis? Charles Anderson resolves several of these problems with an artful, if unverifiable, theory that "the letter from Laodicea" was written by Epaphras (Anderson 1966). This would explain why Paul sends greetings to the Laodiceans in the letter to the Colossians: He himself has not written the Laodiceans. Other scholars have suggested that "the letter from Laodicea" was Ephesians or Philemon. Still others think that it was a genuine Pauline letter that was lost at an early date. A "Letter from Paul to the Laodiceans" was actually preserved by the early church, but it is an obvious forgery (Elliott 1993, 543-46). More important than the issue of the identity of the "letter from Laodicea" is that this proposal to exchange letters is probably the first hint anywhere of a collection of Pauline letters: Letters addressed to one church are assumed relevant to others.

The Archippus mentioned in verse 17 is presumably the same individual mentioned in Phlm 2 as Paul's "fellow soldier" and is associated with the household of Philemon and Apphia. Verse 17 refers to an unspecified ministry that Archippus has received from the Lord and now must fulfill, and it instructs the Colossians to do the admonishing (cf. 3:16). Coming after verses 15-16, this instruction seems to imply that Archippus resides in Laodicea. Perhaps he is the primary Christian leader there, the successor of Epaphras, who can help with the reading and interpretation of the letter to the Colossians. One scholar conjectures that Archippus was really the owner of Onesimus and Paul's meaning here is that Archippus should set his slave free (Knox 1955, 562). Is there in verse 17 an implication that Archippus has faltered in his responsibilities and needs to be encouraged? Presumably the Colossians will know the nature and status of his ministry, and Paul sees no need to elaborate.

Greco-Roman letters often ended with an autograph, a statement in the handwriting of the author after a secretary had written most of the letter. In verse 18 Paul takes the writing instrument from the hand of a scribe and writes a greeting in his own hand. Presumably what he writes are the words that form the whole of 4:18. Similar statements appear in 1 Cor 16:21; Gal 6:11; Phlm 19; 2 Thess 3:17; and Paul may have written a few words in his own handwriting at the conclusions of even the letters that lack such explicit statements. Explicit mention of the autograph, as in 4:18, would be desirable since most Colossian Christians would presumably hear the letter read aloud rather than read it themselves. The autograph would emphasize the authority of the letter-writer probably more than the letter's authenticity (cf. Weima 1994, 127). Perhaps Paul, or the person who writes in his name, inscribes this final greeting in his own hand just to make the letter more personal—without assuming that his readers will have any doubts about his identity or that, if they do, this procedure will eliminate them.

"Remember my chains" recalls the emphasis on Paul's present suffering in 1:24 and imprisonment in 4:3 and the concern that Tychicus and Onesimus report orally on Paul's situation (4:7-9). Not only is Paul presently in prison, he is chained to a wall or perhaps a guard. It is conceivable that there is an allusion to the "bond of love" (see 3:14), since Paul's imprisonment is for the sake of the church. On the other hand, verse 18b is also a final assertion of Paul's integrity as one who suffers for his faithfulness to the gospel, and thus implies his right to be heard in Colossae.

"Grace be with you" is a short but meaningful benediction. These are the very last words in three New Testament letters:

Colossians and 1 and 2 Timothy. Titus ends with "Grace be with all of you." A benediction specifying "the grace of our [the] Lord Jesus [Christ]" closes 1 and 2 Corinthians, Galatians, Philippians, 1 and 2 Thessalonians, and Philemon (cf. Rom 16:20; Eph 6:24). Colossians uses "grace" in two other passages (1:2, 6), in both cases suggesting it refers to the entire force or result of the message concerning Jesus; but it is described in those passages as stemming from God, not Jesus. Thus the customary Christ-linked Pauline way of speaking about grace is found neither at the beginning (1:2) nor the end (4:18) of Colossians.

◊ ◊ ◊ ◊

The final section of the letter offers a window on the early Pauline churches as networks and communities of friends. It is likely that all the persons named in 4:7-17 are church leaders. The church is not a faceless monolith, nor is it a loose association of mystics who have soared beyond human limitations. Paul suggests his own vulnerability and need of others in verse 11, just as he asked for prayers to speak as he ought (vv. 3-4). The Colossians need encouragement in relation to Paul's situation, Mark has not always been reliable, Epaphras must be commended, Archippus needs prodding. "People need one another in the community; even the apostle needs brethren and friends" (Schweizer 1982a, 243).

Paul speaks with authority, even when giving instructions to a church he has not visited: He speaks as one in chains to persons who are also bound to Christ. All or most of the persons who send greetings apparently are members of a missionary team headed by the apostle. Tychicus and Onesimus are sent by him, and yet Paul is not simply their chief; they are his beloved brothers, and their integrity (faithfulness) is what is praised (and this must mean more than simple loyalty to Paul). Paul generally in this passage speaks the language of collegiality, not the language of an authoritarian apostle. Colossians contains no reference to a hierarchy of church offices or apostolic succession, in contrast to the Pastoral Letters (Gnilka 1980, 242). Still, Paul's authority is strongly implied throughout the passage.

Although unknown personally to the Colossians, Paul assumes they will care about him, about his current circumstances, his chains, his being comforted by the presence with him of other Jewish Christians, his appreciation of Luke as a "beloved physician." They are expected to respect his commendation of Epaphras and his now positive words about Mark. The apostle speaks throughout 4:7-18 in the first-person singular (except for a single "we" in v. 8). Timothy seems virtually forgotten, though he might seem to belong in the small band mentioned in 4:11 (but see Cohen 1986).

The demands Paul makes on the Colossians are not outwardly onerous. There are no requests for money, no demands for volunteers to join Paul in prison or in risking martyrdom. There is a strong suggestion that each individual mentioned, whether with Paul or in one of the churches of the Lycus Valley, has a special task or duty. One may see here an extension of one idea underlying 3:18–4:1, that distinctive responsibilities are compatible with the fundamental ending of distinctions in Christ (3:11).

Still, verse 16 implies a momentous demand: This letter to the Colossians must be accepted as an authoritative statement of Christian belief and moral responsibility, and not just by one local church. The primary warrant presented for accepting the letter is, in turn, the personal authority of the apostle, who concludes the letter in his own handwriting (v. 18).

The command to "Remember my chains" is appropriate whether the letter was written by Paul, Timothy, or a later Paulinist. This final admonition reminds the readers that the apostle has carried out his own commission with honor, regardless of obstacles and costs. The Colossians are left to ponder the paradox of a prisoner who confidently proclaims freedom: freedom through Christ from fear of any and all supernatural powers; freedom from guilt and death; and freedom under one final Lord for life in the ordinary world, a world in which Paul's service to that Lord will be continued by a circle of trusted friends.

SELECT BIBLIOGRAPHY

WORKS CITED IN THE TEXT
(EXCLUDING COMMENTARIES)

Adams, David. 1979. "The Suffering of Paul and the Dynamics of Luke–Acts." Ph.D. diss., Yale University.

Anderson, Charles P. 1966. "Who Wrote 'the Epistle from Laodicea'?" *JBL* 85:436-40.

Arnold, Clinton E. 1996. *The Colossian Syncretism: The Interface Between Christianity and Folk Belief at Colossae*. Grand Rapids, MI: Baker.

Attridge, Harold W. 1994. "On Becoming an Angel: Rival Baptismal Theologies at Colossae." In *Religious Propaganda and Missionary Competition in the New Testament World: Essays Honoring Dieter Georgi*, edited by Lukas Bormann et al., 481-98. Leiden: E. J. Brill.

Balch, David L. 1981. *Let Wives Be Submissive: The Domestic Code in 1 Peter*. SBLMS 26. Chico, CA: Scholars Press.

Barclay, John M. G. 1997. *Colossians and Philemon*. New Testament Guides. Sheffield: Sheffield Academic Press.

Barth, Karl. 1956. *The Doctrine of Reconciliation: Church Dogmatics IV/1*. Edinburgh: T & T Clark.

Bassler, Jouette M. 1982. *Divine Impartiality: Paul and a Theological Axiom*. SBLDS 59. Chico, CA: Scholars Press.

Bauer, Walter. 1979. *A Greek-English Lexicon of the New Testament and Other Early Christian Literature*. 2nd ed. Chicago: University of Chicago Press.

Beutler, Johannes. 1994. "Das universale Heil in Christus nach dem Kolosserbrief." *Geist und Leben* 67:403-13.

Billerbeck, Paul. 1926. "Die Briefe des Neuen Testaments und die Offenbarung Johannis. erläutert aus Talmud und Midrasch." In *Kommentar zum Neuen Testament aus Talmud und Midrasch*, 3. Munich: Beck.

Bockmuehl, Markus N. A. 1990. *Revelation and Mystery in Ancient Judaism and Pauline Christianity.* WUNT 2. Reihe, 36. Tübingen: Mohr-Siebeck.

Bornkamm, G. 1975. "The Heresy of Colossians." In *Conflict at Colossae.* Rev. ed., edited by Fred O. Francis and Wayne A. Meeks, 123-45. Missoula, MT: Scholars Press.

Broekhoven, Harold Van. 1997. "The Social Profiles in the Colossian Debate." *JSNT* 66:73-90.

Bujard, W. 1973. *Stilanalytische Untersuchungen zum Kolosserbrief als Beitrag zur Methodik von Sprachvergleichen.* SUNT 11. Göttingen: Vandenhoeck & Ruprecht.

Cannon, G. E. 1983. *The Use of Traditional Materials in Colossians.* Macon, GA: Mercer University Press.

Carr, Wesley. 1981. *Angels and Principalities.* SNTSMS 42. Cambridge: Cambridge University Press.

Cohen, Shaye J. D. 1986. "Was Timothy Jewish (Acts 16:1-3? Patristic Exegesis, Rabbinic Law, and Matrilineal Descent." *JBL* 105:251-68.

Collins, Matthew. 1995. "Rhetoric, Household and Cosmos: A Rhetorical and Sociological Analysis of the Letter to the Colossians with Particular Focus on Col 3:18–4:1." Ph.D. thesis, Vanderbilt University.

Conzelmann, Hans. 1979. "Die Schule des Paulus." In *Theologia Crucis—Signum Crucis: Festschrift Erich Dinkler,* edited by C. Andresen and G. Klein, 85-96. Tübingen: Mohr-Siebeck.

Crouch, James E. 1972. *The Origin and Intention of the Colossian Haustafel.* FRLANT 109. Göttingen: Vandenhoeck & Ruprecht.

Dahl, Nils A. 1976. *Jesus in the Memory of the Early Church.* Minneapolis: Augsburg.

D'Angelo, Mary Rose. 1994. "Colossians." In *Searching the Scriptures: A Feminist Commentary,* edited by E. Schüssler Fiorenza, 313-24. New York: Crossroad.

de Boer, Martinus C. 1980. "Images of Paul in the Post-Apostolic Period." *CBQ* 42:359-80.

DeMaris, Richard E. 1994. *The Colossian Controversy: Wisdom in Dispute at Colossae.* JSNTSup 96. Sheffield: JSOT.

Dibelius, M. 1975. "The Isis Initiation in Apuleius and Related Initiatory Rites." In *Conflict at Colossae.* Rev. ed., edited by Fred O. Francis and Wayne A. Meeks, 61-121. Missoula, MT: Scholars Press.

Elliott, J. K. 1993. *The Apocryphal New Testament: A Collection of*

Apocryphal Christian Literature in an English Translation. Oxford: Clarendon.

Fitzgerald, John T. 1992. "Virtue/Vice Lists." *ABD* 6:857-59.

Francis, F. O. 1975a. "Humility and Angelic Worship in Colossae." In *Conflict at Colossae.* Rev. ed., edited by Fred O. Francis and Wayne A. Meeks, 163-95. Missoula, MT: Scholars Press.

Francis, Fred O. 1975b. "The Background of *embateuein* (Col 2:18) in Legal Papyri and Oracle Inscriptions." In *Conflict at Colossae.* Rev. ed., edited by Fred O. Francis and Wayne A. Meeks, 197-207. Missoula, MT: Scholars Press.

———. 1977. "The Christological Argument of Colossians." In *God's Christ and His People: Studies in Honour of Nils Alstrup Dahl,* edited by Jacob Jervell and Wayne A. Meeks, 192-208. Oslo: Universitetsforlaget.

Furnish, Victor Paul. 1992. "Colossians, Epistle to the." *ABD* 1.1090-96.

Gabathuler, H. J. 1965. *Jesus Christus. Haupt der Kirche—Haupt der Welt. Der Christushymnus Kolosser 1,15-20 in der theologischen Forschung der letzten 130 Jahre.* Zurich: Zwingli.

Gager, John. 1975. *Kingdom and Community: The Social World of Early Christianity.* Englewood Cliffs, NJ: Prentice-Hall.

Gibbs, J. G. 1971. *Creation and Redemption: A Study in Pauline Theology.* NovTSup 26. Leiden: E. J. Brill.

Gielen, M. 1986. "Zur Interpretation der paulinischen Formen *he kat oikon ekklesia* [the house church]." *ZNW* 77:109-25.

Goulder, Michael. 1995. "Colossians and Barbelo." *NTS* 41:601-19.

Hamerton-Kelly, Robert G. 1973. *Pre-Existence, Wisdom and the Son of Man: A Study of the Idea of Pre-Existence in the New Testament.* Cambridge: Cambridge University Press.

Hartman, Lars. 1985. "Universal Reconciliation (Col 1.20)." *SNT(SU)* 10:109-21.

———. 1995. "Humble and Confident: On the So-Called Philosophers in Colossians." In *Mighty Minorities? Minorities in Early Christianity—Positions and Strategies: Essays in Honour of Jacob Jervell on His 70th Birthday 21 May 1995,* edited by David Hellholm, Halvor Moxnes, Turid Karlsen Seim, 25-39. Oslo: Scandinavian University Press.

Hay, David M. 1997. "Pauline Theology After Paul." In *Pauline Theology Volume IV: Looking Back, Pressing On,* edited by E. Elizabeth Johnson and David M. Hay, 181-95. SBL Symposium Series. Atlanta: Scholars Press.

Hegermann, H. 1961. *Die Vorstellung vom Schöpfungsmittler im hellenistischen Judentum und Urchristentum* TU 82. Berlin: Akademie Verlag.

Holladay, Carl. 1995. *Fragments from Hellenistic Jewish Authors: Volume III Aristobulus.* Atlanta: Scholars Press.

Hooker, Morna D. 1973. "Were There False Teachers at Colossae?" In *Christ and Spirit in the New Testament: Essays in Honour of C. F. D. Moule,* edited by B. Lindars and S. S. Smalley, 315-31. Cambridge: Cambridge University Press.

Hoppe, Rudolf. 1994. *Der Triumph des Kreuzes: Studien zum Verhältnis des Kolosserbriefes zur paulinischen Kreuzestheologie.* SBB 28. Stuttgart: Verlag Katholisches Bibelwerk.

Hurtado, Larry W. 1988. *One God, One Lord: Early Christian Devotion and Ancient Jewish Monotheism.* Philadelphia: Fortress.

Jervell, Jacob. 1960. *Imago Dei: Gen 1.26f. im Spätjudentum, in der Gnosis und in den paulinischen Briefen.* FRLANT 58. Göttingen: Vandenhoeck & Ruprecht.

Johnson, Sherman E. 1950. "Laodicea and Its Neighbors." *BA* 13/1:1-18.

Julian of Norwich. 1978. *Showings.* New York: Paulist.

Käsemann, Ernst. 1964. "A Primitive Christian Baptismal Liturgy." In Käsemann, *Essays on New Testament Themes.* SBT 41, 149-68. Naperville, Ill: Allenson.

Kehl, N. 1967. *Der Christushymnus im Kolosserbrief: Eine motivgeschichtliche Untersuchung zu Kol 1,12-20.* Stuttgart: Katholisches Bibelwerk.

Knox, John. 1955. "The Epistle to Philemon." *IB* 11:553-73.

Kremer, Jacob. 1956. *Was an den Leiden Christi noch mangelt: Eine interpretationsgeschichtliche und exegetische Untersuchung zu Kol. 1,24b.* BBB 12. Bonn: Peter Hanstein.

Lähnemann, Johannes. 1971. *Der Kolosserbrief: Komposition, Situation und Argumentation.* SNT 3. Gütersloh: Gerd Mohn.

Layton, Bentley. 1987. *The Gnostic Scriptures.* Garden City, NY: Doubleday.

Lesses, Rebecca M. 1998. *Ritual Practices to Gain Power: Angels, Incantations, and Revelation in Early Jewish Mysticism.* HTS 44. Harrisburg, PA: Trinity Press International.

Lona, Horacio E. 1984. *Die Eschatologie im Kolosser—und Epheserbrief.* Würzburg: Echter Verlag.

Malherbe, Abraham J. 1977. *The Cynic Epistles.* SBLSBS 12. Missoula, MT: Scholars Press.

Martin, Troy, 1995. "The Scythian Perspective in Col. 3.11." *NovT* 37:249-61.

Martin, Troy W. 1996. *By Philosophy and Empty Deceit: Colossians as a Response to a Cynic Critique.* JSNTSup 118; Sheffield: Sheffield Academic Press.

Meeks, Wayne A. 1977. "In One Body: The Unity of Humankind in Colossians and Ephesians." In *God's Christ and His People: Studies in Honour of Nils Alstrup Dahl,* edited by Jacob Jervell and Wayne A. Meeks, 209-21. Oslo: Universitetsforlaget.

―――. 1983. *The First Urban Christians: The Social World of the Apostle Paul.* New Haven, CT: Yale University Press.

―――. 1993. " 'To Walk Worthily of the Lord': Moral Formation in the Pauline School Exemplified by the Letter to Colossians." In *Hermes and Athena: Biblical Exegesis and Philosophical Theology,* edited by Eleonore Stump and Thomas P. Flint, 37-58. Notre Dame, IN: University of Notre Dame Press.

Metzger, Bruce M. 1964. *The Text of the New Testament.* New York and London: Oxford University Press.

Neumann, Kenneth J. 1990. *The Authenticity of the Pauline Epistles in the Light of Stylostatistical Analysis.* Atlanta: Scholars Press.

Newsom, Carol. 1985. *Songs of the Sabbath Sacrifice: A Critical Edition.* HSS. Atlanta: Scholars Press.

Nielsen, Charles M. 1985. "The Status of Paul and His Letters in Colossians." *Perspectives in Religious Studies* 12:103-22.

Nock, Arthur Darby. 1959. "Posidonius." In *JRS* 49:1-15.

Norden, Eduard. 1923. Reprint 1956. *Agnostos Theos: Untersuchungen zur Formengeschichte Religiöser Rede.* Darmstadt: Wissenschaftliche Buchgesellschaft.

O'Brien, Peter T. 1977. *Introductory Thanksgivings in the Letters of Paul.* NovTSup 49. Leiden: E. J. Brill.

Olbricht, Thomas H. 1996. "The Stoichcia and the Rhetoric of Colossians: Then and Now." In *Rhetoric, Scripture and Theology: Essays from the 1994 Pretoria Conference,* edited by Stanley E. Porter and Olbricht, 308-28. Sheffield: Sheffield Academic Press.

Ollrog, Wolf-Henning. 1979. *Paulus und seine Mitarbeiter: Untersuchungen zu Theorie und Praxis der paulinischen Mission.* WMANT 50. Neukirchen-Vluyn: Neukirchener Verlag.

Osiek, Carolyn, and David L. Balch. 1997. *Families in the New Testament World: Households and House Churches.* Louisville: Westminster John Knox.

Percy, Ernst. 1946. *Die Probleme der Kolosser— und Epheserbriefe.* Lund: C. W. K. Gleerup.

Perkins, Pheme. 1997. *Ephesians.* ANTC. Nashville: Abingdon.

Robinson, James M. 1957. "A Formal Analysis of Colossians 1:15-20." *JBL* 76:270-87.

Runia, David T. 1986. *Philo of Alexandria and the Timaeus of Plato.* Philosophia Antiqua 44. Leiden: E. J. Brill.

Sappington, Thomas J. 1991. *Revelation and Redemption at Colossae.* JSNTSup 53. Sheffield: JSOT.

Schenk, W. 1987. "Der Kolosserbrief in der neueren Forschung (1945–1985)." *ANRW* II.25.4: 3327-64. Berlin: de Gruyter.

Schenke, Hans-Martin. 1964. "Der Widerstreit gnostischer und kirchlicher Theologie im Spiegel des Kolosserbriefes." *ZTK* 61:391-403.

Schrage, Wolfgang. 1990. *The Ethics of the New Testament.* Philadelphia: Fortress.

Schubert, Paul. 1939. *Form and Function of the Pauline Thanksgivings.* BZNW 20. Berlin: Töpelmann.

Schussler Fiorenza, Elisabeth. 1984. *In Memory of Her: A Feminist Theological Reconstruction of Christian Origins.* New York: Crossroad.

Schweizer, Eduard. 1973. "Christus und Geist in Kolosserbrief." In *Christ and Spirit in the New Testament,* edited by B. Lindars and S. S. Smalley, 297-313. Cambridge: Cambridge University Press.

———. 1982b. *Neues Testament und Christologie im Werden: Aufsätze.* Göttingen: Vandenhoeck & Ruprecht.

———. 1988. "Slaves of the Elements and Worshipers of Angels: Gal 4:3, 9 and Col 2:8, 18, 20." *JBL* 107:455-68.

Standhartinger, Angela. 1999. *Studien zur Entstehungsgeschichte und Intention des Kolosserbriefs.* NotTSup 94. Leiden: E. J. Brill.

Sterling, Gregory E. 1998. "A Philosophy According to the Elements of the Cosmos: Colossian Christianity and Philo of Alexandria." In *Philon d'Alexandrie et la langage de la philosophie,* edited by Carlos Lévy, 349-73. Turnhout, Belgium: Brepols.

Stuckenbruck, Loren T. 1995. *Angel Veneration and Christology.* WUNT 2. Reihe, 70. Tübingen: Mohr-Siebeck.

Sumney, Jerry. 1993. "Those Who 'Pass Judgment': The Identity of the Opponents in Colossians." *Bib* 74:366-88.

Taylor, Walter F., Jr. 1992. "Unity/Unity of Humanity." *ABD* 6.746-53.

Theiler, Willy. 1982. *Poseidonios: Die Fragmente.* 2 vols. Berlin: DeGruyter.

Walter, Nikolaus. 1979. "Die Handscrift in Satzungen Kol 2:14." ZNW 70:115-18.

Wedderburn, A. J. M. 1993. "The Theology of Colossians." In *The Theology of the Later Pauline Letters,* edited by Andrew T. Lincoln and A. J. M. Wedderburn, 3-71. New Testament Theology. Cambridge: Cambridge University Press.

Weima, Jeffrey A. D. 1994. *Neglected Endings: The Significance of the Pauline Letter Closings.* JSNTSup 101. Sheffield: JSOT.

Weiss, Herold. 1972. "The Law in the Epistle to the Colossians." CBQ 34:294-314.

Williamson, Lamar, Jr. 1968. "Led in Triumph: Paul's Use of *Thriambeuo.*" Int 22:317-32.

Wilson, Walter T. 1994. *The Mysteries of Righteousness: The Literary Composition and Genre of the Sentences of Pseudo-Phocylides.* TSAJ 40. Tübingen: Mohr-Siebeck.

———. 1997. *The Hope of Glory: Education and Exhortation in the Epistle to the Colossians.* NovTSup 88. Leiden: E. J. Brill.

Winston, David. 1979. *The Wisdom of Solomon.* AB 43. Garden City, NY: Doubleday.

Wright, N. T. 1990. "Poetry and Theology in Colossians 1.15-20." NTS 36:444-68.

COMMENTARIES (BOTH CITED AND NOT CITED)

Abbott, T. K. 1897. *Epistles to the Ephesians and to the Colossians.* ICC. Edinburgh: T. & T. Clark.—A still-important commentary on the Greek text, emphasizing issues of vocabulary and syntax. The arguments of Baur and Holtzmann against Pauline authorship are discussed and rejected. Valuable detailed notes on patristic and modern interpretations.

Aletti, Jean-Noel. 1993. *Saint Paul: Épitre aux Colossiens.* Paris: J. Gabalda.—Detailed commentary on Greek text. Paul was probably the author. Emphasizes rhetorical analysis of the letter and argues that it is the earliest Christian writing to emphasize the union of Christ and his church.

Barth, Markus, and Helmut Blanke. 1994. *Colossians.* AB 34B. Garden City, NY: Doubleday.—After publishing his two-volume Anchor Bible commentary on Ephesians in 1974, Barth began work on this commentary but died (in 1994) before completing it. The final work on it was done by his doctoral student (Blanke) and Astrid Beck. The result is an uneven work that at some points offers only sketchy comments, but at others presents detailed and insightful discussions of the text and major interpretations. Favors Paul as author.

Bruce, F. F. 1984. *The Epistles to the Colossians, to Philemon, and to the Ephesians.* NICNT. Grand Rapids, MI: Eerdmans.—A careful conservative analysis of the flow of thought in the letter, with detailed comments on Greek terms and historical issues in footnotes. Paul wrote the letter from Rome. The Colossian "heresy" may have been an early form of Jewish Merkabah mysticism.

Conzelmann, H. 1965. "Der Brief an die Kolosser." *Die Briefe an die Römer und an die Korinther, Die kleineren Briefe des Apostles Paulus,* 131-56. NTD (10. Aufl.) Bd. III. Göttingen: Vandenhoeck & Ruprecht.—A brief (twenty-five page) commentary offering perceptive comments on theological ideas in the letter and affinities with other Pauline letters. Authorship question is left open. The opponents are Gnostics.

Dibelius, Martin, and Heinrich Greeven. 1953. *An die Kolosser, Epheser, an Philemon.* HNT 12. Tübingen: Mohr-Siebeck.—One of the major commentaries of recent times, despite its brevity. Its notes on Jewish and pagan background materials are remarkable for fullness and discrimination. The Colossian Error was a syncretistic movement with links to pagan mystery religions, Judaism, and Gnosticism.

Donelson, Lewis R. 1996. *Colossians, Ephesians, 1 and 2 Timothy, and Titus.* Westminster Bible Companion. Louisville: Westminster John Knox.—A brief readable commentary based on the NRSV and designed for lay readers. The letter was written by a Pauline disciple who wove Pauline ideas into a new theological vision. The core problem at Colossae was the threat of cosmic powers opposed to Christ.

Dunn, James D. G. 1996. *Commentary on Colossians and Philemon.* NIGTC. Grand Rapids, MI: Eerdmans.—An outstanding full commentary on the Greek text, which summarizes much recent scholarship. Timothy probably wrote the letter on Paul's behalf. The Colossian "Error" was simply a local form of nonsyncretistic Judaism.

Gnilka, Joachim. 1980. *Der Kolosserbrief.* HTKNT 10:1. Freiburg: Herder & Herder.—A major commentary in the German tradition. The letter is from the Pauline school in Ephesus.

Harris, M. J. 1991. *Colossians and Philemon.* Exegetical Guide to the Greek New Testament. Grand Rapids, MI: Eerdmans.—A commentary that consists mainly of notes on vocabulary and syntax of the Greek text. Bibliographies on relevant scholarly literature and homiletical suggestions from an evangelical perspective fill out the brief guide.

Hübner, H. 1997. *An Philemon. An die Kolosser. An die Epheser.* HNT 12. Tübingen: Mohr-Siebeck.—A concise commentary that emphasizes the theological meaning of the letter, with some discussion of recent scholarship and textual issues. Comparative background material receives much less attention than in the older HNT volumes (like that of Dibelius-Greeven). The letter is pseudonymous. The Colossian "philosophy" was syncretistic, but it cannot be reconstructed in detail from the letter's ambiguous references.

Lightfoot, J. B. 1884. Reprint 1995. *Saint Paul's Epistles to the Colossians and to Philemon.* Peabody, MA: Hendrickson.—One of the great nineteenth-century commentaries. Still valuable for its notes on Greek terminology. Paul wrote the letter to combat a false teaching linked with the Essenes.

Lindemann, A. 1983. *Der Kolosserbrief.* Zürcher Bibelkommentare: NT 10. Zürich: Theologischer Verlag.—Brief but offers historically and theologically acute comments on the flow of thought in the letter. A Pauline disciple wrote the letter, actually intending it for the Laodicean church. It is a very carefully crafted systematic presentation. The Colossian Error was a mix of Jewish, Christian, Gnostic and mystery religion features.

Lohmeyer, Ernst. 1964. *Die Briefe an die Kolosser und an Philemon.* MeyerK 13. Aufl.; Göttingen: Vandenhoeck & Ruprecht.—A classic technical commentary essentially completed in 1929. It is an authentic Pauline letter, and Paul's suffering as an early Christian witness-martyr is emphasized, as well as his use of the Christ hymn in Col 1:15-20. The false teaching in Colossae was a form of Gnosticism with a Jewish background, one that encouraged self-salvation.

Lohse, Eduard. 1971. *Colossians and Philemon.* Hermeneia. Philadelphia: Fortress.—One of the most important technical commentaries on the Greek text (all Greek terms are explained, however). Particularly strong discussions of connections with Jewish backgrounds, including the Dead Sea Scrolls. The letter is a powerful new formulation of Pauline ideas by a member of the Pauline school to counter a form of syncretistic "philosophy" with Jewish and pre-Gnostic features.

Martin, Ralph P. 1985. *Colossians and Philemon*. New Century Bible Commentary. Grand Rapids, MI: Eerdmans.—A short commentary based on the Revised Standard Version. There are valuable notes on key issues of interpretation. Martin finds no strong evidence against Pauline authorship.

Moule, C. F. D. 1957. *The Epistles to the Colossians and Philemon*. CGTC. Cambridge: Cambridge University Press.—An outstanding, pithy commentary on the Greek text, which emphasizes linguistic difficulties and theological issues. Paul wrote the letter.

O'Brien, Peter T. 1982. *Colossians, Philemon*. WBC 44. Waco: Word.—A detailed conservative commentary on the Greek text, with extensive discussion of various scholarly opinions. Paul was the real author, though he may have relied on a colleague like Timothy for the actual writing. The Error was a blend of Jewish and pagan elements.

Pokorný, Petr. 1991. *Colossians: A Commentary*. Peabody, MA: Hendrickson.—A major commentary by a Czech scholar, who, among other things illuminates the letter's ethical teaching by references to the difficulties of living as a Christian in a modern secularized society. Major historical and theological issues are emphasized, as is the flow of argumentation. The letter is pseudonymous. The Error was a syncretistic movement resembling later Gnosticism.

Reumann, John H. P. 1985. "Colossians." In *Ephesians and Colossians*, edited by Walter F. Taylor, Jr. and John H. P. Reumann. ACNT. Minneapolis: Augsburg.—A short, readable commentary, with valuable notes on recent scholarship. A Pauline disciple wrote the letter soon after 70 CE. We cannot precisely know the nature of the Colossian Error.

Schweizer, Eduard. 1982a. *The Letter to the Colossians: A Commentary*. Minneapolis: Augsburg.—One of the best and most influential of recent commentaries, with detailed discussion of all major theological issues and important notes on the history of interpretation. Timothy wrote the letter while Paul was imprisoned. The key to understanding the Colossian Error is a Pythagorean text of the first-century BCE.

Thurston, Bonnie. 1995. *Reading Colossians, Ephesians and 2 Thessalonians: A Literary and Theological Commentary*. New York: Crossroad.—A short nontechnical commentary. Paul probably wrote the letter.

Wolter, Michael. 1993. *Der Brief an die Kolosser. Der Brief an Philemon*. Ökumenischer Taschenbuchkommentar zum Neuen

Testament. Bd. 12. Gütersloh: Gerd Mohn.—A brief commentary offering challenging historical and theological insights. A Paulinist wrote the letter after the apostle's death.

Wright, N. T. 1986. *The Epistles of Paul to the Colossians and to Philemon—An Introduction and Commentary*. Tyndale New Testament Commentaries 12; Grand Rapids, MI: Eerdmans.—A concise commentary written for a popular audience. Paul wrote the letter to warn ex-pagans against Judaism. Christ has taken the position that was assigned to the Mosaic law by Judaism.

Yates, Roy. 1993. *The Epistle to the Colossians*. London: Epworth.—A lively, short commentary on the English text. A member of a Pauline school in Ephesus wrote the letter. The Error was a form of Jewish mysticism moving in the direction of Gnosticism.

INDEX